WORTHING
THROUGH TIME
Sally White

AMBERLEY PUBLISHING

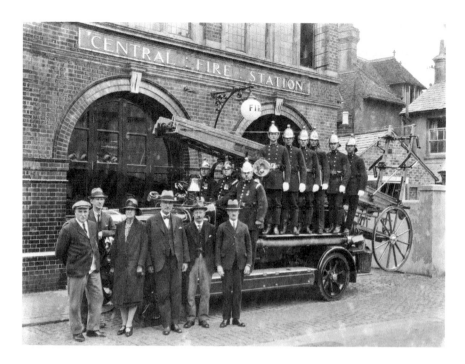

Showing Off Their Fine Fire Engine
The Central Fire Station was built in the High Street in about 1905 and stood where Crown House is now. Taken *c.* 1925, this picture shows Councillor Eliza Knight of Knight's Dairy in the High Street surrounded by firemen. They are standing proudly in front of their motor-driven fire engine. In the early 1960s, the fire station moved to the edge of Broadwater from where it still operates.

I lived in Worthing and worked at the Museum for twenty years from 1984. I am very grateful to the people who welcomed me, talked to me about their town and their lives, encouraged me in my curiosity and made my time there so rewarding. It was a privilege and this book is for them.

First published 2009

Amberley Publishing Plc
Cirencester Road, Chalford,
Stroud, Gloucestershire, GL6 8PE

www.amberley-books.com

Copyright © Sally White, 2009

The right of Sally White to be identified as the Author of this work has been asserted in accordance with the Copyrights, Designs and Patents Act 1988.

ISBN 978 1 84868 124 8

British Library Cataloguing in Publication Data.
A catalogue record for this book is available from the British Library.

Typeset in 9.5pt on 12pt Celeste.
Typesetting by Amberley Publishing.
Printed in the UK.

Introduction

I have a deep affection for Worthing; a town I first visited over half a century ago when I was two and which has pulled me back repeatedly. I can, therefore, claim to have known it 'through time' and have certainly seen many changes, both good and bad. Although still seen by some people as a backwater, Worthing has always reflected the state of the country as a whole. In the 1860s, when the resort was thriving, it was quick to add the latest in seaside attractions, a pier. In the 1920s, the elegant bandstand was replaced by a far more modern Band Enclosure, later to become the Lido. Like any other town, Worthing suffered in the 1960s from the tendency to demolish buildings that many people thought should be saved, and to replace them with blank-faced brick or concrete monstrosities like the bowling alley and car park on the old Grafton House site or like Teville Gate. On the whole, Worthing flourished in the 1980s-90s. At the moment, the number of empty shops and reduced expenditure reflect the economic situation of the country as a whole. Economic ups and downs are a part of history and there is no doubt that in time the shops will again be full, the streets busy and the town will regain a more optimistic air.

Worthing remained quite a small resort town until the late nineteenth century when the fact that it was possible to commute weekly, or even daily, to London by train led many people to settle here. After the First World War, development speeded up with ribbon development reaching north up Findon Valley and bungalows being built in huge numbers in Goring and around the edges of the town. Looking at the old photographs, it is clear how many rural or semi-rural areas were swallowed up by Worthing at this time.

Semi-affectionate nicknames such as 'the elephants' graveyard' persist, but don't do the town justice. It does, indeed, have a high percentage of elderly residents, but it is far more than a retirement town where everyone in the rest of the country seems to have an aged relative. It is a home to many families. Some have lived here for generations, contributing to the development of the town. Others have been brought here more recently by work or other reasons, often beguiled by all the town has to offer into staying longer than they had originally intended to.

What I did not realise when I agreed to write this book was just how difficult it would be to take some of the modern photographs. I had to find a day and time when there would be people around but when the streets would not be clogged with cars and I had to dodge traffic, climb walls and balance on traffic islands in order to get the views I wanted! It made me realise just how much street lamps, bollards, parking meters, signposts, flower displays, railings, benches and adverts have filled our pavements and verges. These all add to the feeling of business in many of the modern photographs and are in stark contrast to the more open views of the older pictures. They must also make navigating the streets a nightmare for anyone who has poor eyesight, who depends on a wheelchair or who is pushing a child in a buggy.

Worthing Library has an amazing collection of old photographs and continues to add to it, making them available through the West Sussex Past Website. The recent addition of the archive from Walter Gardiner Photography is invaluable. This firm has been in Worthing since 1893, chronicling the town and its people. During the Second World War, they were able to take photographs of areas forbidden to most people and this part of the archive is particularly interesting. Many of the photographs in this book are taken from their collection.

Worthing is an attractive and appealing town, happily sandwiched between the English Channel and the beautiful countryside of the South Downs and within easy reach of the more cosmopolitan attractions of Brighton and London. It has a great deal to offer both residents and visitors alike. Worthing has a rich and fascinating history and I hope this glimpse of how the town has changed over the years will stimulate memories, inform and entertain you whether your roots are deeply embedded in Sussex or whether you are just getting to know the town.

Sally White
November 2009

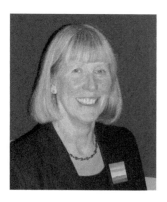

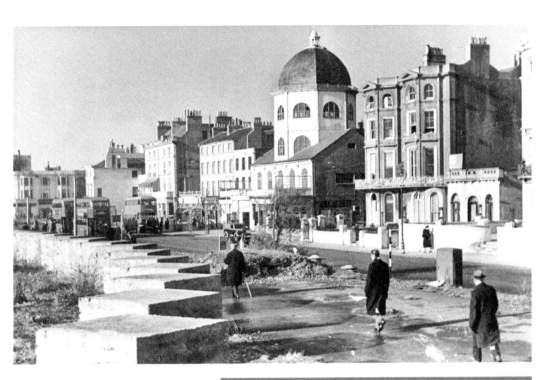

The Dome in Wartime
The Dome, Worthing's Edwardian cinema, looks lost behind the concrete 'tank traps' that were put along the seafront during the Second World War to prevent a German invasion. Removing the blocks and other defences from across the area was a major and very expensive task at the end of the war. The Dome still operates as a cinema and is a much-loved icon of the Worthing seafront.

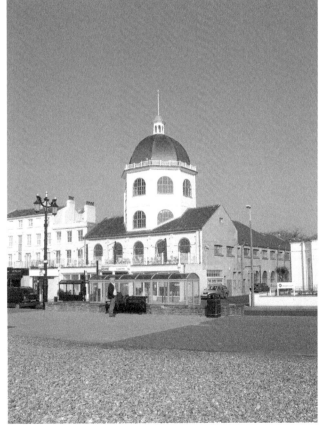

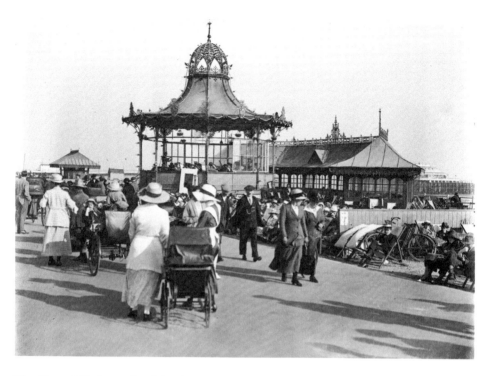

The Elegant Birdcage Bandstand
The birdcage bandstand and shelters were demolished in 1925 to make way for the Band Enclosure. It had been the site for hundreds of popular band concerts, but tastes were changing. Although the Lido has been very popular in its turn, the seafront would be more attractive if it still had its elegant bandstand and if music from the brass bands still wafted over the seafront. This picture was taken in c. 1917.

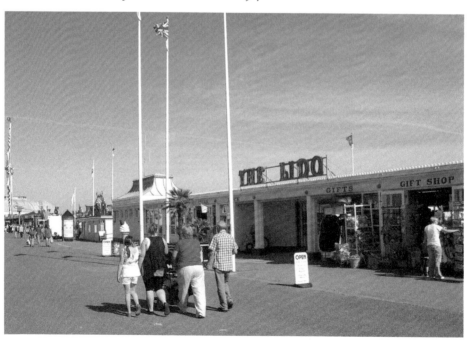

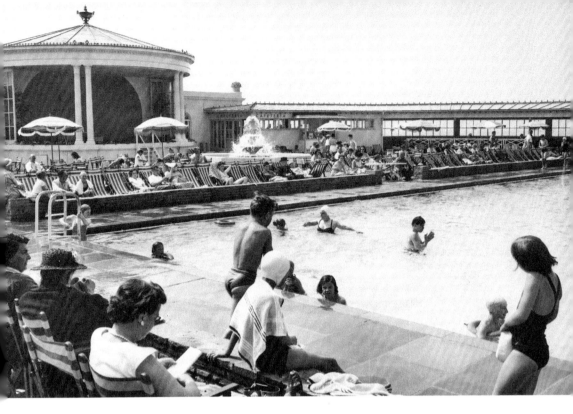

The Lido with Swimming Pool and Bandstand

The smart new Band Enclosure opened in 1926. It was spacious and very modern in design. This picture was taken in *c.* 1957 when it was renamed the Lido after the addition of an unheated swimming pool in front of the bandstand. The pool was covered over when concerts took place. Today, the pool and the regular band concerts are all in the past, but it is still a popular entertainment centre, with café, shops and rides for children.

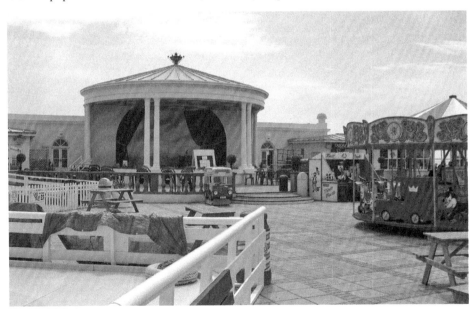

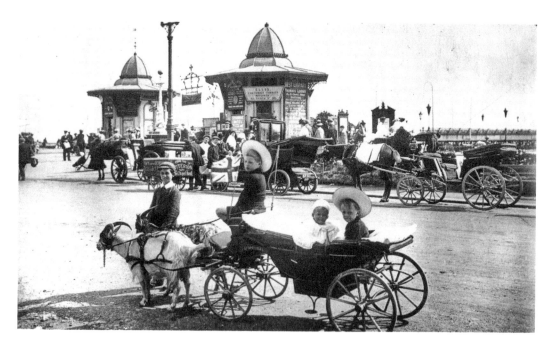

Goat Carriage in Front of the Pier

Small carriages pulled by goats used to be a feature of Worthing seafront, but would not be allowed today. The kiosks at the entrance to the Pier were built in 1914, when the Pier reopened after suffering huge damage in a storm. One was the tollbooth and the other, a 'fancy repository'. In the 1920s, they were replaced by the solid Pier Pavilion and entrance we know today where concerts of all sorts take place.

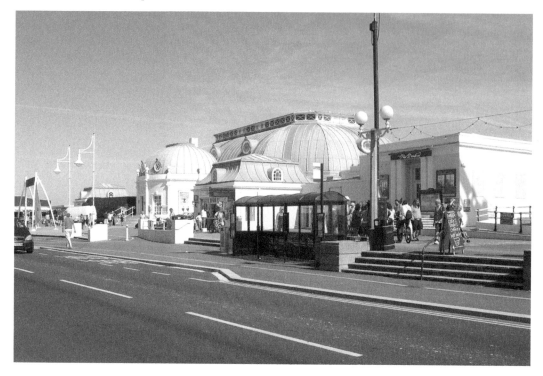

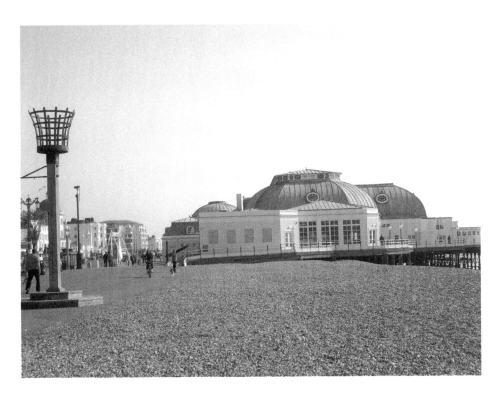

Out of Bounds!

Worthing promenade has an open, relaxing feel to it today. In this wartime picture, it is almost unrecognisable. When we hear that the seafront was covered in barbed wire to prevent a German invasion, few people picture the incredible quantity of coiled wire shown in this picture. Laying and later removing it must have been a nightmare for the soldiers asked to do it. The military trucks parked beside the promenade were American.

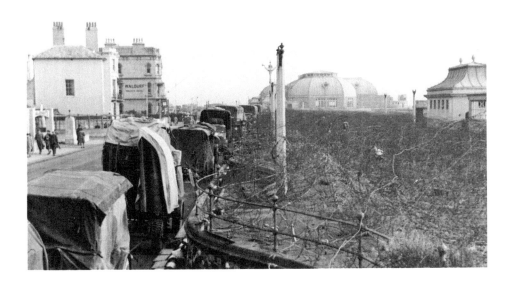

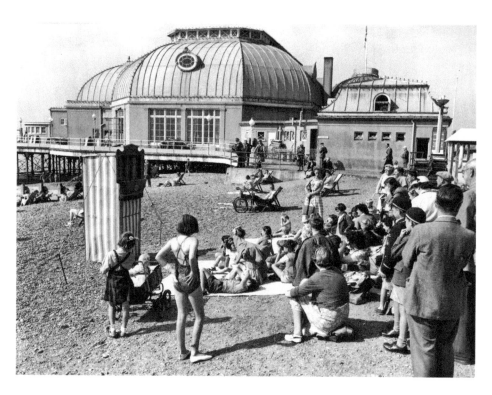

Entertainment 1950s Style

The Pier has been the focus of all sorts of entertainment over the years. Most recently, it has hosted the annual Birdman competition. In the 1950s, a Punch and Judy Show was performed regularly just to the east of the Pavilion. Much earlier, this was the site of Worthing's fish market. A seasonal tourist information centre, a small information display and a few small fishing boats now occupy the site.

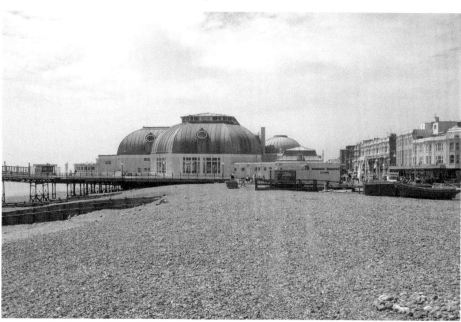

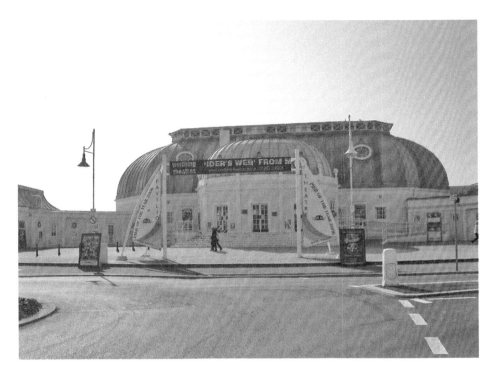

The Framework Hidden Inside the Pavilion

The Council has installed banners and a digital advertising display in front of the Pavilion, possibly in an attempt to soften its somewhat heavy appearance. The pavilion design was controversial from the start, but this unusual picture of its construction in 1925 shows the elaborate iron framework that was needed to give it its rounded shape. The workmen don't look busy. Perhaps the wet weather had stopped them working.

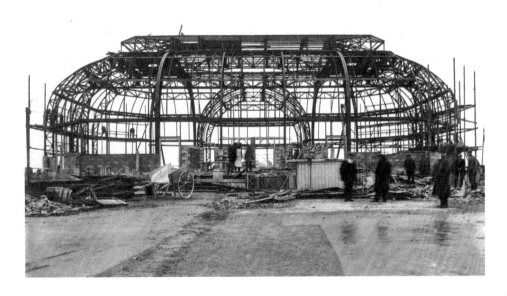

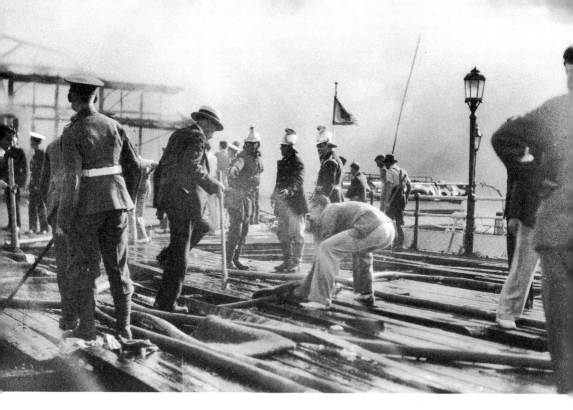

All Hands to the Pump!

Worthing Pier is the only pier to have been blown down, burnt down and blown up, and after each disaster, it was quickly rebuilt with modern additions. In this 1933 photograph members of public can be seen trying to salvage the decking from the burning pier. They started this while waiting for the fire brigade to arrive. The central Amusement Pavilion was built after the fire and opened in 1939, not long before a hole was blown in the Pier to prevent a German landing.

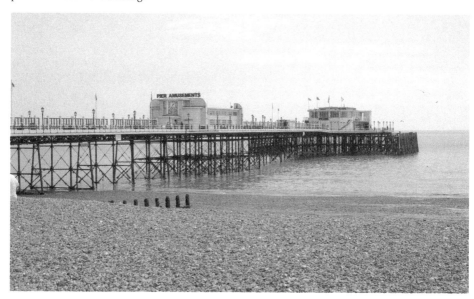

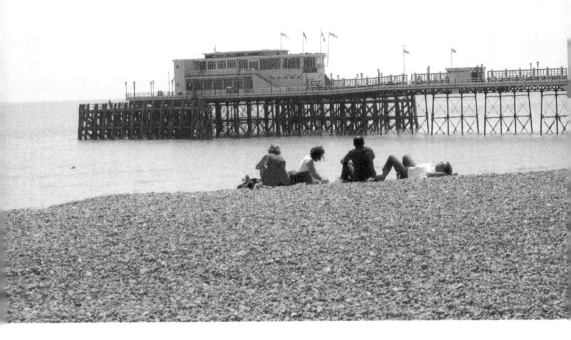

Where Better to Relax with Friends?

The beach is the ideal place to relax, to sit and chat with friends, to admire the Pier and to be lulled by the waves landing on the shingle. In the late nineteenth century, bathing was done, in voluminous costumes, from one of the many bathing machines which were for hire. Modesty was all-important, in sharp contrast to today.

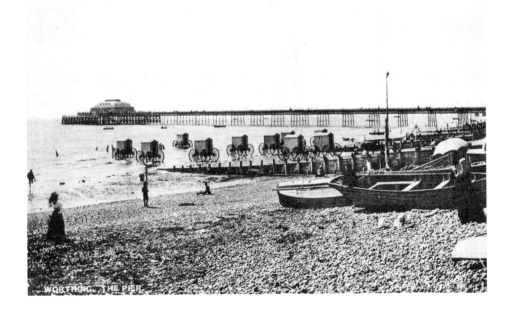

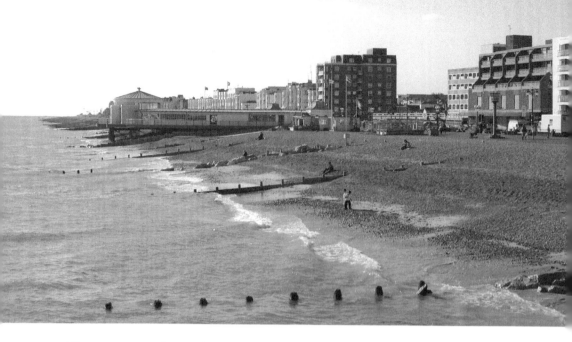

The Western Beach Seen from the Pier

For years we were told that the British seaside holiday is a thing of the past. With the current recession, many more people are choosing to try the delights offered by modern resorts. Even so, as this September picture shows, the western part of the beach was almost empty once the school holidays had ended. The Edwardian picture shows crowds of people in elaborate and all-covering clothes, enjoying the beach. The birdcage bandstand is in the background.

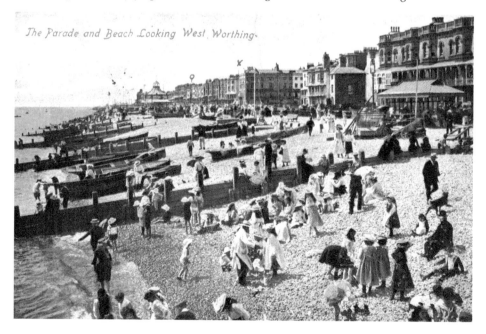

The Parade and Beach Looking West, Worthing.

Fast Food and Summer Weather
Cool drinks on a hot day have long
been popular, as shown by these
ladies sampling Mr Gibbs' fruit
and fruit juice on Marine Parade
to the west of the Pier in c. 1900.
The buildings behind them, on the
corner of Montague Place, have
changed little over the years. For
many decades, Worthing Council
has boasted about the town's good
weather, but the skies were not
always blue this summer as the
lowering clouds in this picture show.

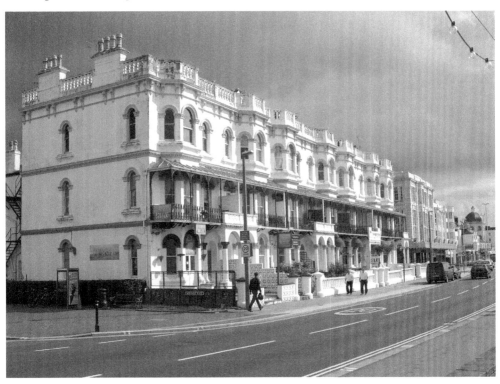

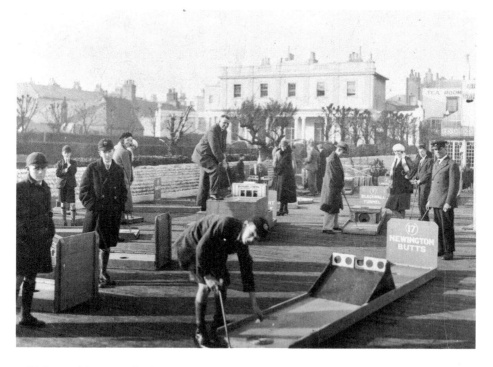

Which Would You Prefer?

The car park and bowling alley on the seafront are almost universally described as hideous and there have been a number of plans for developing the plot of land in front, none of which has materialised. The bowling alley is on the site formerly occupied by the elegant Grafton House, while the plots in front have been used for various entertainments, including Hewitt's funfair and the miniature golf course, shown here in *c.* 1930.

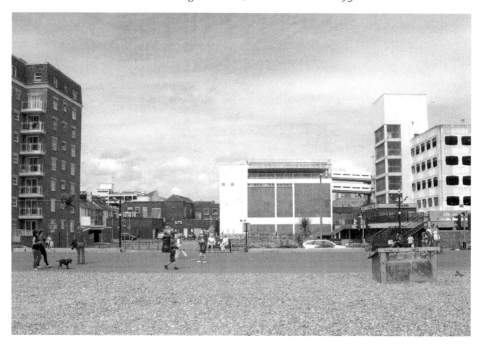

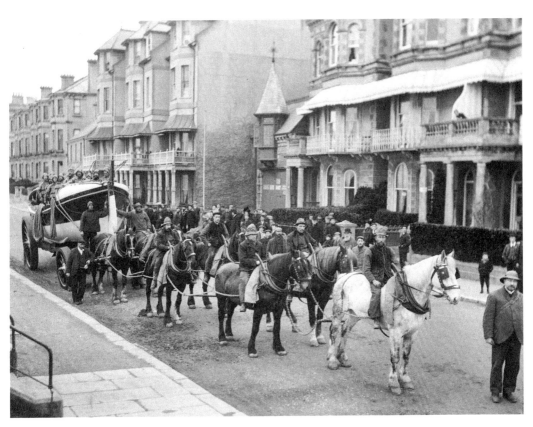

The Lifeboat and Lifeboat House

The former Lifeboat House on Marine Parade is now remarkable only for its pointed turret. There is no sign of the important role it used to play as the base for the Worthing lifeboat. For many years, the lifeboat was a vital support for local fishermen and other sailors in the Channel. Volunteering as lifeboat men ran in a number of Worthing families.

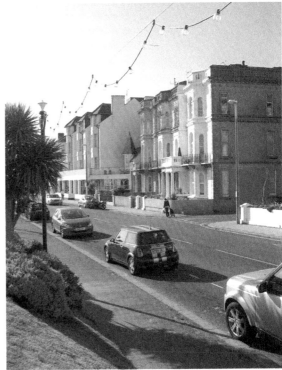

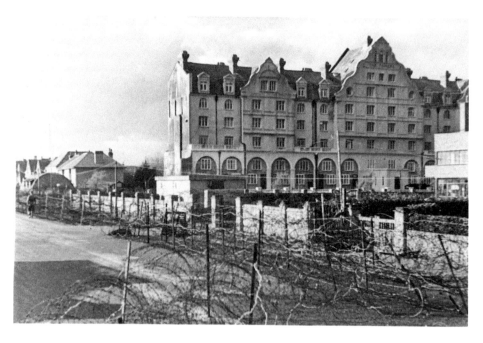

Worthing's 'White Elephant', The Towers

A soldier is patrolling the barbed wire barrier on the West Worthing seafront near the isolated block of The Towers in *c*. 1944. Since this picture was taken, The Towers has been renamed Dolphin Lodge and has had a modern block attached to its southern face. The Towers was designed as a grand hotel, part of a larger scheme, which was never completed. Instead, The Towers was made into elegant flats.

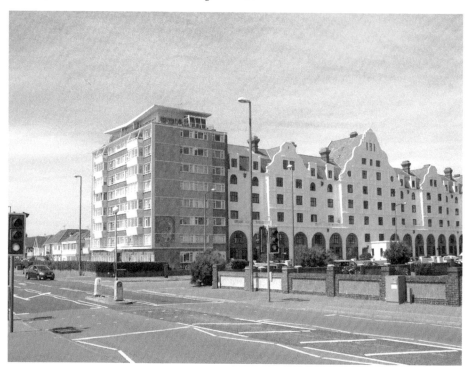

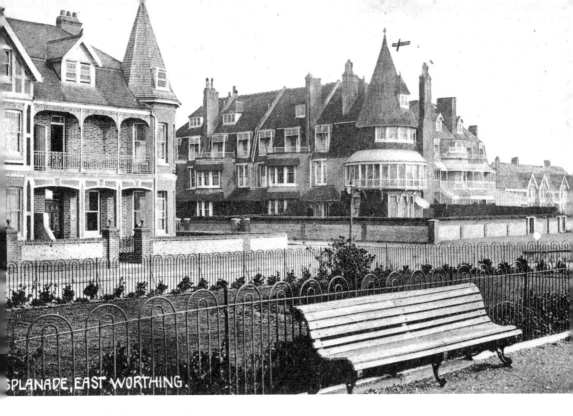

ESPLANADE, EAST WORTHING.

Oscar Wilde's Temporary Home

It is easy to imagine Oscar Wilde writing *The Importance of Being Earnest* in the turreted room he rented at The Haven, 5 The Esplanade in 1894. While he was here, he presented the prizes at the annual Regatta. Sadly, this elegant building was demolished and replaced by a stark block of flats and a garage. A blue plaque is the only indication of the role this site played in the life of one of our great writers.

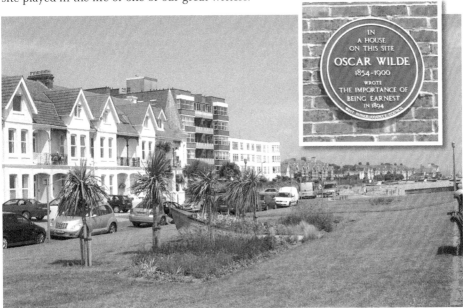

IN A HOUSE ON THIS SITE
OSCAR WILDE
1854-1900
WROTE
THE IMPORTANCE OF BEING EARNEST
IN 1894

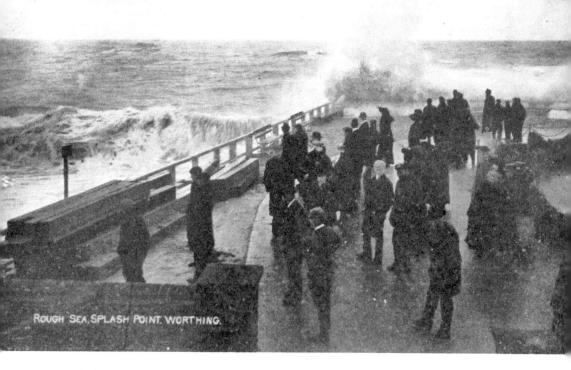

ROUGH SEA, SPLASH POINT, WORTHING.

Enjoying Splash Point

Splash Point, at the eastern end of the promenade, was aptly named and crowds often gathered there to watch the waves breaking over the seafront, as in this photograph of *c.* 1910. In recent years, boulders have been heaped on the beach to reduce the force of the waves and Splash Point is a much more tranquil spot than it used to be.

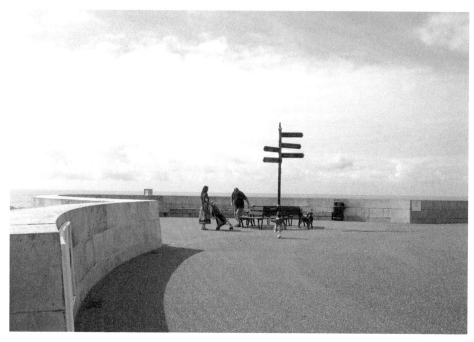

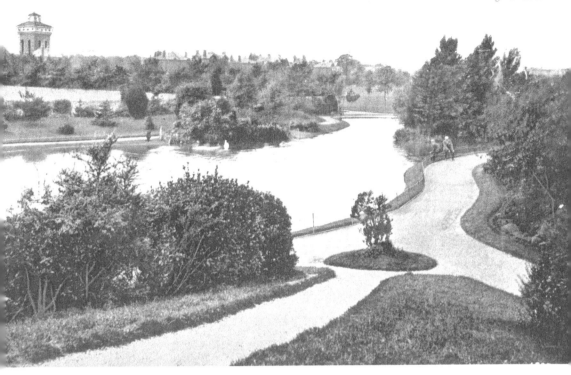

The People's Park

Set up in the Victorian period, Homefield Park was originally called the People's Park. It was laid out with a lake, paths, flowerbeds and wooded areas. Today, it is much simpler and overshadowed by the modern hospital but it is still popular with groups of all ages. The lake has been filled in but there is a playground, café and open grassy areas as well as the skateboard park.

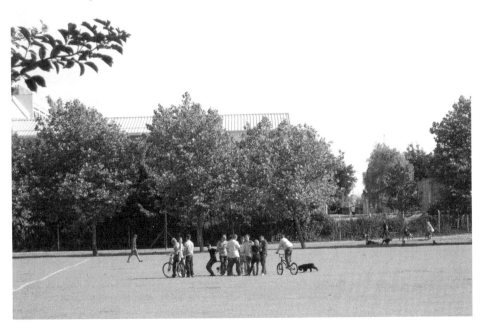

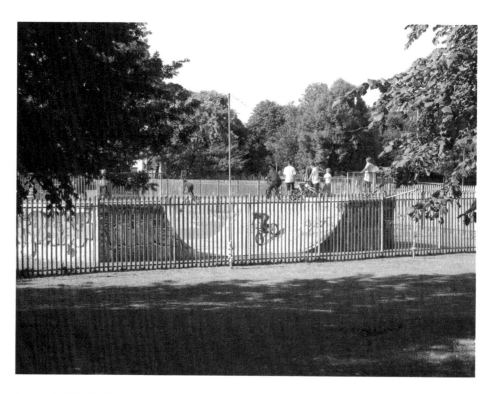

Sports In The Park

Sports and exercise have long been popular in Homefield Park. Groups of young people, mostly boys, gather in the skateboard park to perform elaborate stunts and to test and develop their skills in front of their peers. Sports Day in 1897 was a more formal affair. The wooden pushchair in the foreground is a complete contrast to the multi-terrain buggies modern parents use.

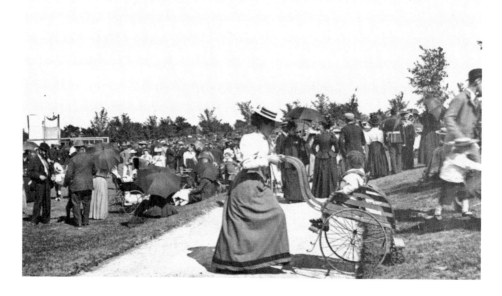

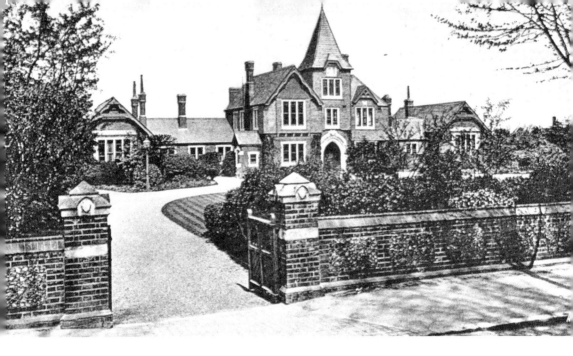

Worthing Hospital

The Infirmary was built in 1881 with only eighteen beds, although a children's ward and an operating theatre were soon added. It was renamed Worthing Hospital in 1904. The original building, shown here, survived until the 1980s when it was demolished to make way for larger modern facilities. Although the new hospital is brighter and much more comfortable, some people were sorry that its construction meant that we had to lose the old buildings.

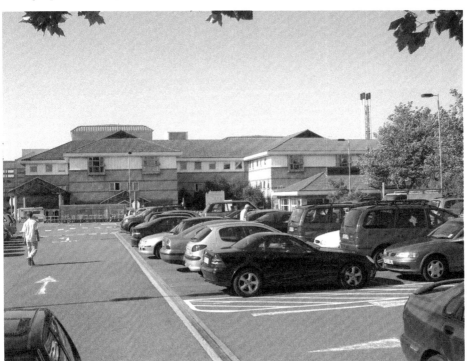

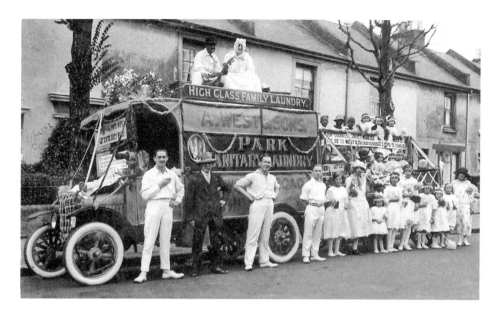

Ready for the Carnival Parade

There were a number of carnivals in Worthing in the early twentieth century and there is nothing to say which one this group was going to parade in. West & Sons, who ran a local laundry, were using the wagon as a float. Take away the float, and the terraced houses in Newlands Road look much the same today as they did in the 1920s.

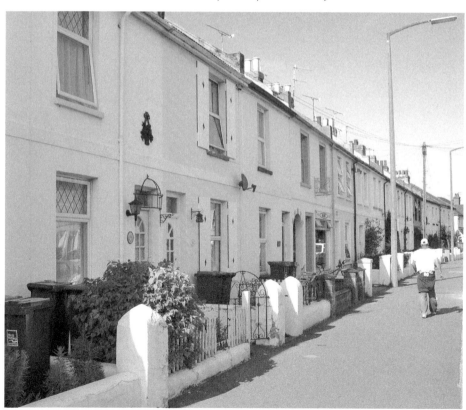

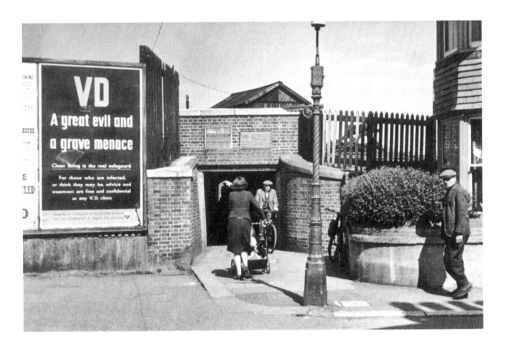

A Warning You Could Not Miss!

During the Second World War posters, like this one warning about the dangers of venereal diseases (VD) were quite common. The billboard is at the northern entrance to Ivy Arch Tunnel, which leads under the railway line. The modern picture shows that the tunnel is still in regular use, although the site of the billboard is now overgrown. There would be plenty of comments today if prominent signs about VD were put up.

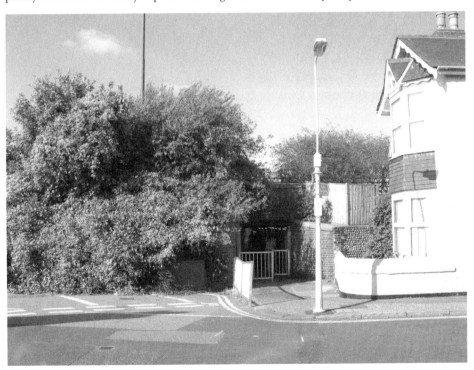

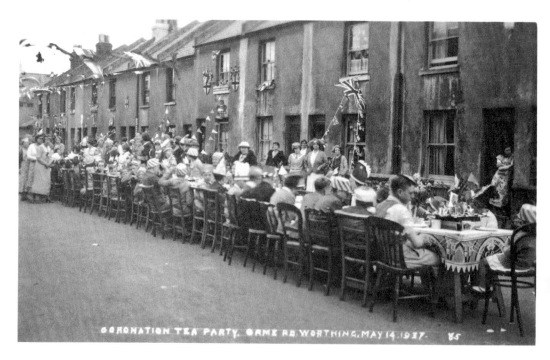

CORONATION TEA PARTY. ORME RD. WORTHING. MAY 14. 1937. 85

Celebrating the End of the War

Street parties are a popular way of celebrating major royal events. This one was held in Orme Road, to mark the Coronation of King George VI on 14 May 1937. It looks as though every child in Orme Road has joined in, while the women have organised the party. Today, the houses are brightly painted in a variety of colours, making the street look much more attractive than it used to.

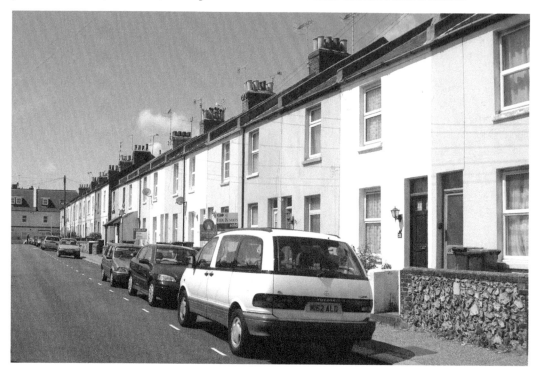

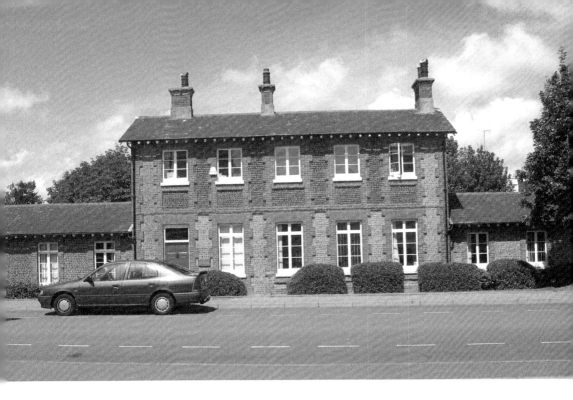

Worthing's First Station

Few people realise that the attractive brick office building at the quiet end of Railway Approach was the first Worthing Station. The railway reached Worthing in 1845 and was soon carrying both commuters and holidaymakers to and from London in large numbers. The tall chimney at the left end of the building has been removed. Note the tall stovepipe hats worn by the office staff on this photograph from the 1870s.

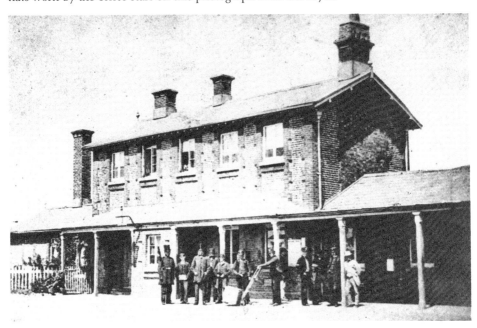

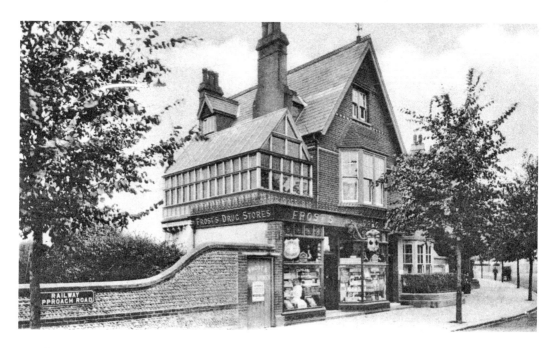

Frost's Drug Stores
The glass gallery on the side of the Edwardian building gives Frost's Drug Stores in Railway
Approach the appearance of a folly. The building has been altered over the years. The chimneys
have been removed and the gallery has been replaced by a solid brick extension. It now houses
several businesses including garage and courier services.

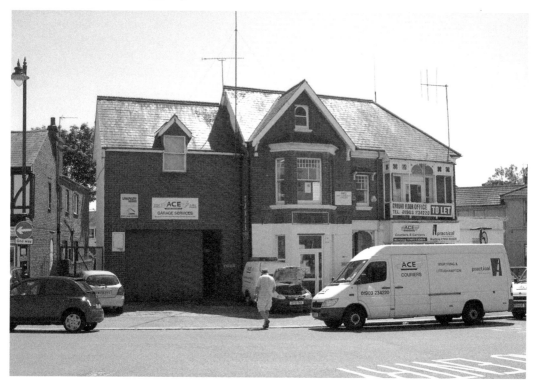

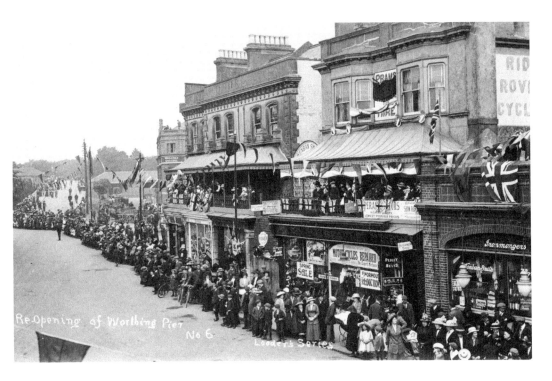

Re.Opening of Worthing Pier No.6 Looder's Series

Changed Beyond Recognition

The north-eastern part of Chapel Road is now dull and unwelcoming but, in May 1914, the shopkeepers had decorated their premises with flags and bunting. Crowds had turned out to greet the Lord Mayor of London who had come down to reopen the Pier, which had been restored after suffering storm damage the previous year. Little did they know that within two months the country would be at war. The railway bridge can be seen in the distance

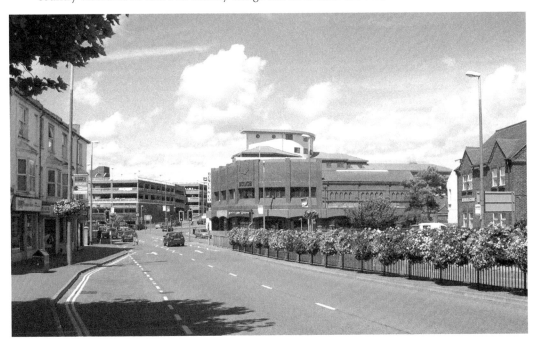

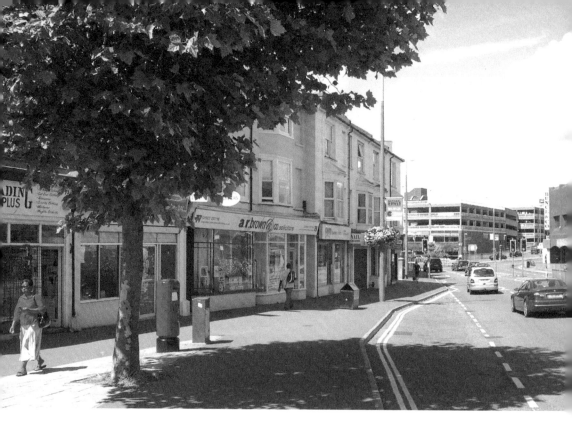

Still Standing but Updated

The north-western part of Chapel Road retains many of its older buildings, still used as shops, but with much brighter facades. The ball on top of the old Rivoli cinema, since demolished, can be seen in the distance of the older picture. Teville Gate multi-storey car park can be seen in the background of the modern photograph. Teville Gate is overdue for redevelopment but there has been a seemingly endless debate about what to do on the site.

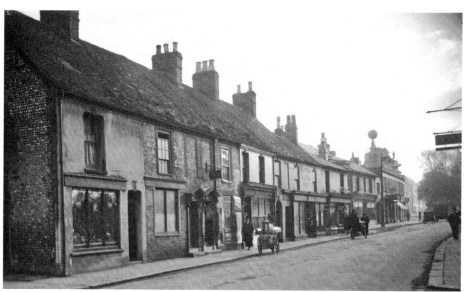

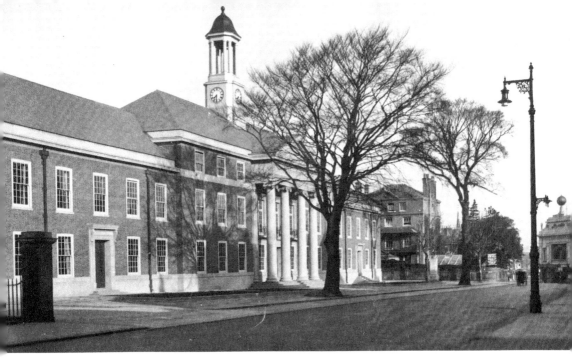

The Essence of Civic Solidity
Worthing's impressive neoclassical Town Hall was opened in 1933. In the background are the Home of the Holy Rood, and the Rivoli cinema, now both replaced by modern buildings. The Town Hall was designed by C. Cowles Voysey and opened in 1933. It has stood the test of time remarkably well. Successive councils have had the sense to keep the area around the Town Hall clear of clutter so that its elegance can still be appreciated.

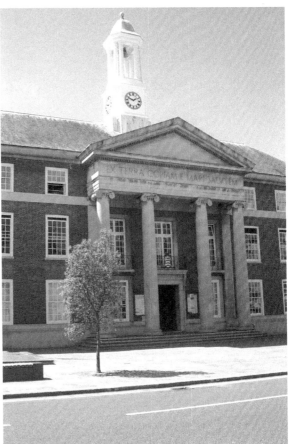

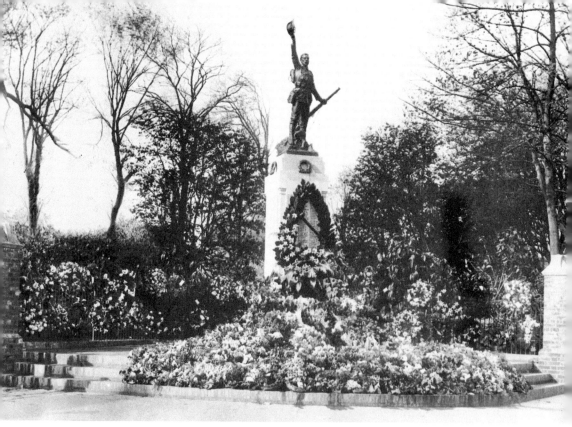

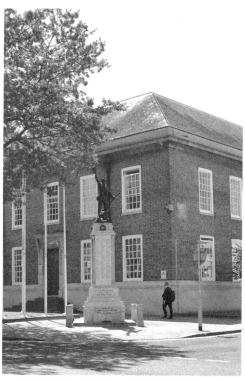

The Newly Unveiled War Memorial

The War Memorial was installed in a brick-built enclosure on the corner of Chapel Road and Stoke Abbott Road in 1921. This picture was taken soon after the unveiling, with many of the flowers that had been laid in tribute to the people who had died in the First World War. The Town Hall was built near the memorial in 1933 and the brick enclosure was removed. It is now at a busy junction instead of being on a quiet corner.

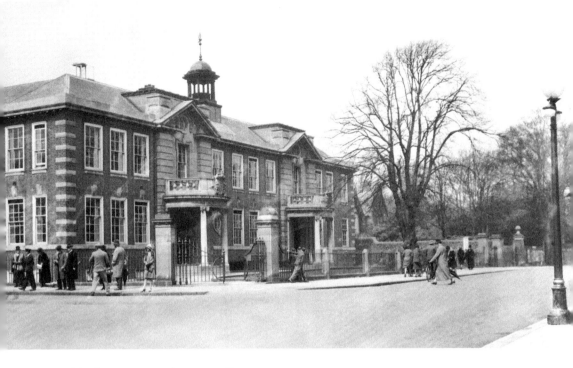

Worthing's Museum and Former Library

One building in two halves was how the Library and Museum were built next to the Town Hall in 1908. They were partly financed by the Scottish philanthropist Andrew Carnegie and local benefactor Alfred Cortis. The iron railings, which enclosed them, were melted down during a wartime salvage drive. In the 1970s, a new library was built around the corner and the Museum has expanded to occupy most of the building.

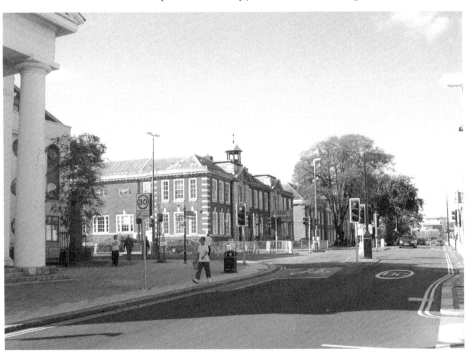

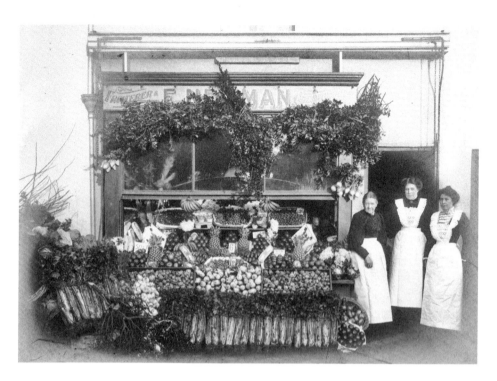

Newman's Fruit and Vegetable Shop, Richmond Road

The eastern end of Richmond Road has changed beyond recognition. Newman's fruit and vegetable shop, seen here in 1895, was one of a row of small shops and cottages along the northern side. The last of these buildings was demolished to make way for council offices. Portland House opened in 1991 and cost £2.7 million. It is now under threat as is the Council, working ever closer with Adur Council needs less space and more money.

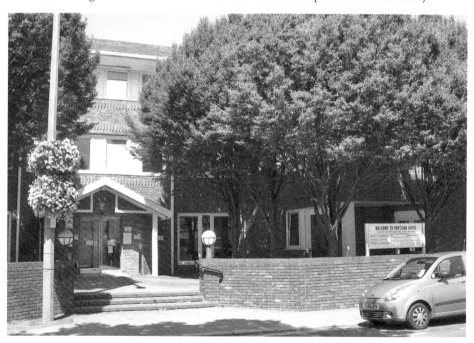

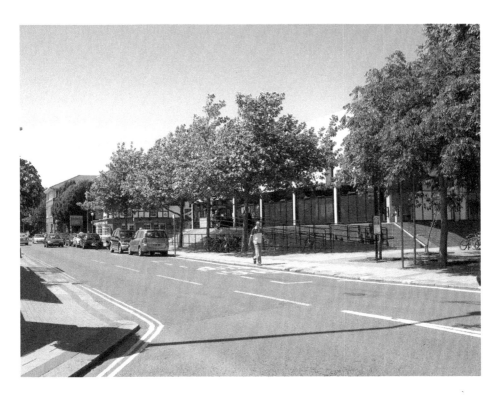

Formerly a Quiet Residential Street

All the old buildings between the mock-Tudor Wheatsheaf public house in Richmond Road and the Museum were demolished. For years, the site was used as a car park, but in 1975, an excellent public library was built on the site. The trees along the pavement have grown fast and now largely obscure the library.

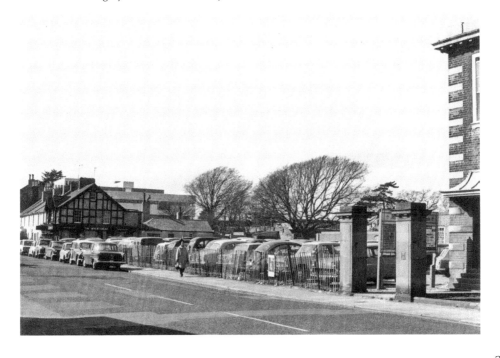

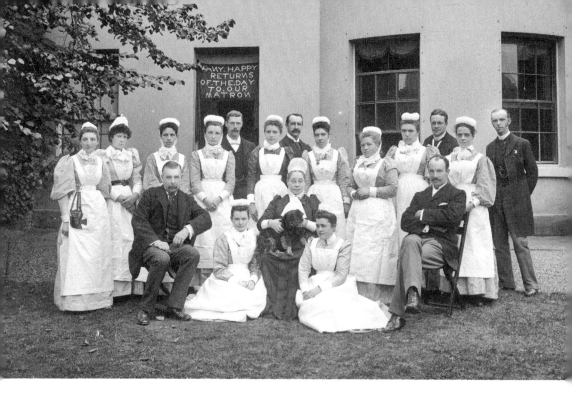

Happy Birthday Matron!

Contaminated drinking water caused a typhoid epidemic in 1893 and a temporary fever hospital was set up in a house in Richmond Road. According to the sign in the window, the staff assembled to celebrate the Matron, Mrs Horton's birthday. She is seated, with her dog on her lap, in the middle of her staff. The gracious house was built in *c.* 1845. It has been well cared for and is now used as a nursery school.

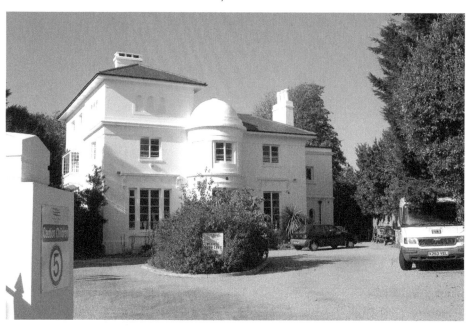

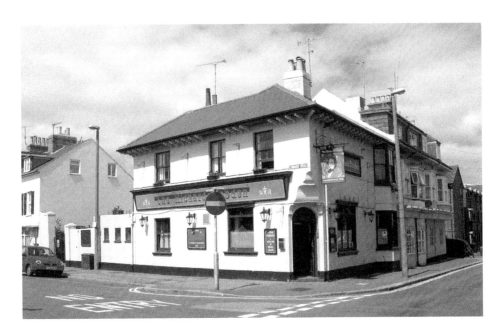

Preparing to Celebrate the Coronation

The Richard Cobden public house, named after the Victorian political campaigner, still stands on the corner of Clifton and Cobden Roads. Unlike many Worthing pubs, it has kept its original name. This picture shows the pub decorated in celebration of the coronation of King George V in 1911. The crowd outside look solemn rather than celebratory and are being watched by a woman in one of the upstairs windows.

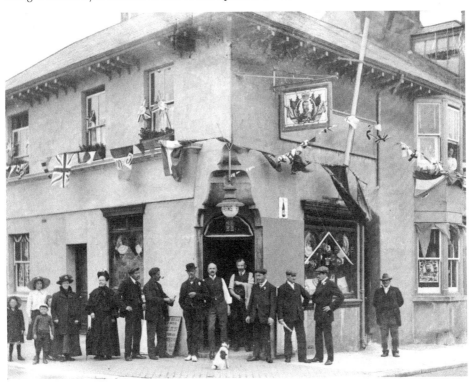

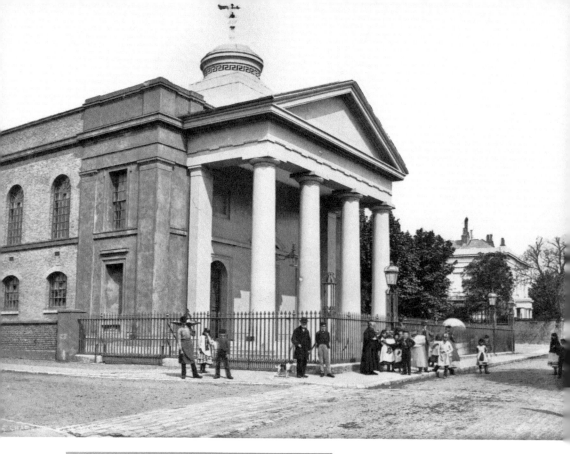

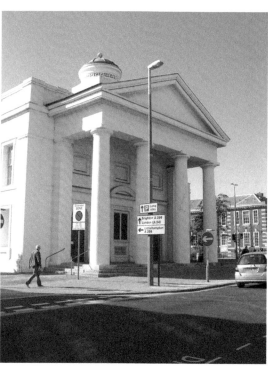

St Paul's Church

St Paul's Church was in built on the corner of Ambrose Place in 1812 as a Chapel of Ease. It has an imposing façade and was originally enclosed by iron railings, but they were removed years ago. Over time, the church became increasingly dilapidated but it has recently been restored so that it looks as good as new. At the time of the restoration, a pleasing hall was built on its northern side for use as a community centre.

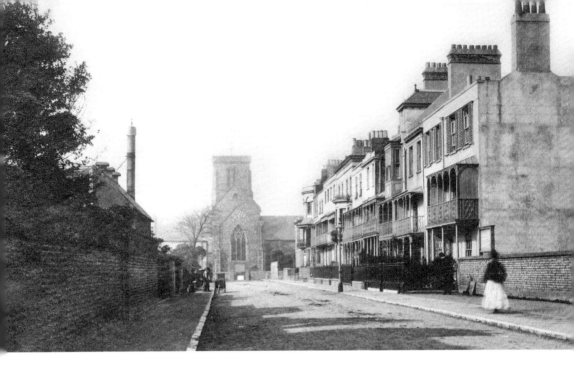

Ambrose Place's Elegant Tranquillity

Ambrose Place has elegant early-nineteenth-century houses along its northern side with gardens on the opposite side of the road. It has changed very little since this picture was taken, apart from an extension to St Paul's Church, added in 1893, and the construction of a solid shop and office building on the south-west corner. It is still one of the most desirable streets in town and the writer Harold Pinter once lived there.

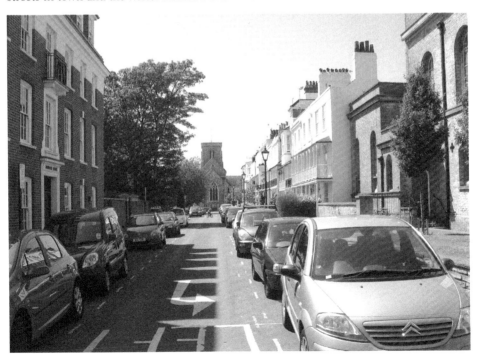

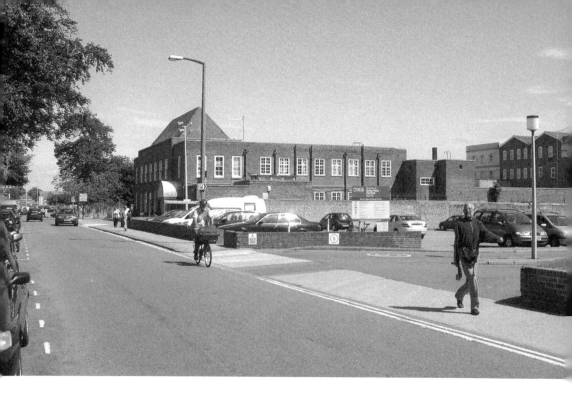

From Car Salesroom to Car Park

Dutton-Forshaw had their showroom and garage in Union Place, between the Connaught Theatre and the police station. After this picture was taken in the 1970s, the garage was demolished, presumably with an eye to redevelopment of the site. No building took place and the site has been used as a car park ever since. The police station is now empty, as the police have moved to smaller premises in Chatsworth Road.

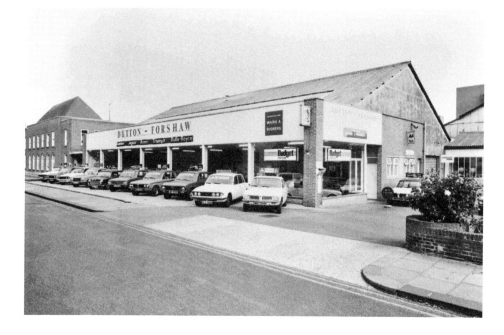

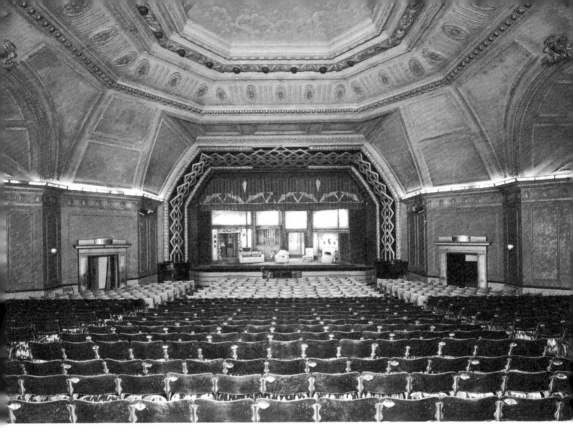

The Connaught

The Art Deco façade of the Connaught Theatre that was built in Union Place in 1914. In a way, its role has gone full circle. It was originally built as a cinema called the Picturedrome. In 1935, it was taken over as a theatre by the Worthing Repertory Company and it was renamed the Connaught Theatre. This picture shows the stage set for a performance in the late 1930s. In 1987, new projection equipment was added and now it serves as both theatre and cinema.

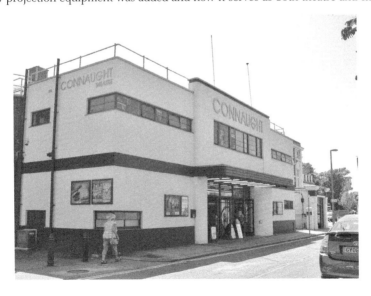

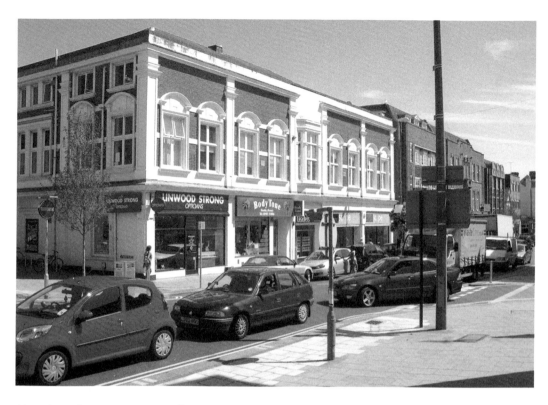

Chapel Road Seen From St Paul's

Superficially, this view of Chapel Road has not changed much. An optician, estate agent and various shops, with modern frontages occupy the Chapel Road building that housed the Connaught Hall, Picturedrome and Kandy's Café in 1925.

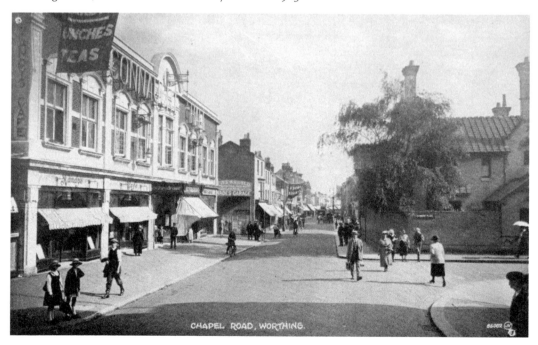

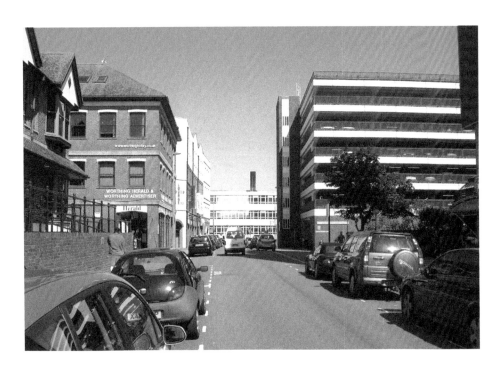

Another World, Not Just a Different Age

Looking east along Chatsworth Road today, with the imposing modern buildings of the Guildbourne Centre and Southern Water on the right and shops, offices and the police station on the left, it is impossible to imagine how it looked little over a hundred years ago. Then, it was known as Cook's Row and consisted of a row of small, run-down, flint cottages and workshops. It was rebuilt and renamed in 1903.

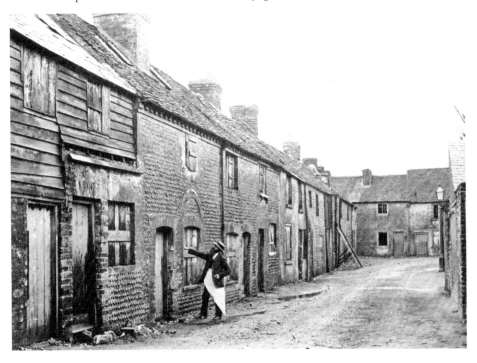

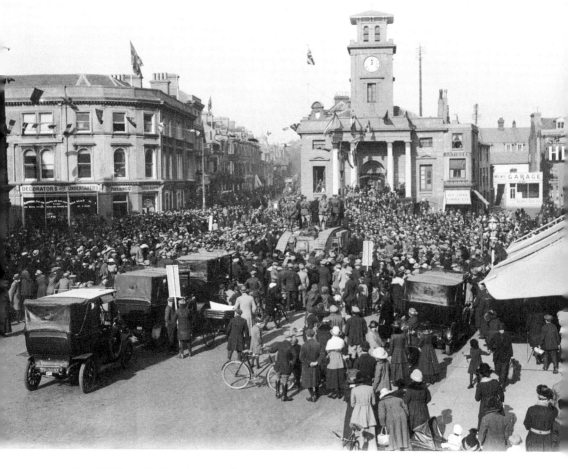

The Old Town Hall and the Tank

Worthing's first town hall was in South Street. Many important civic events took place outside the building. Crowds gathered there to welcome a tank that had been given to the town in recognition of the money raised locally during the 1914-18 war. The tank later stood outside the station and was melted down during the Second World War. The Guildbourne Centre stands on the site today, with a busy taxi rank beside it.

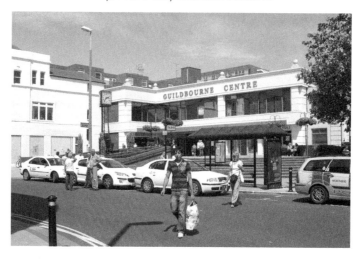

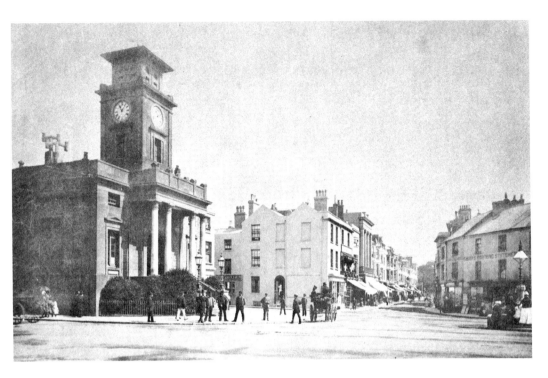

Warwick Street and the Old Town Hall
This once simple and elegant area of the town is now surrounded by busy shops and noisy traffic. Healthy trees and pots of colourful flowers decorate the pedestrian precinct. The older picture shows how the Town Hall was set back from the road with Warwick Street beyond it.

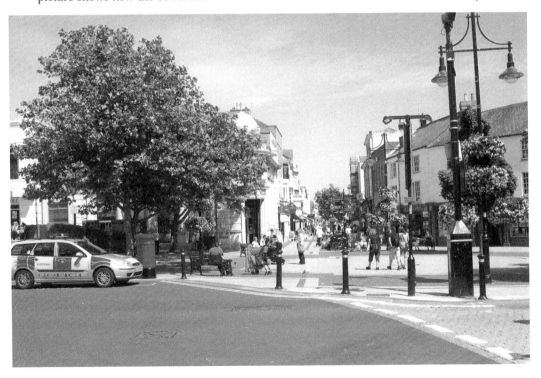

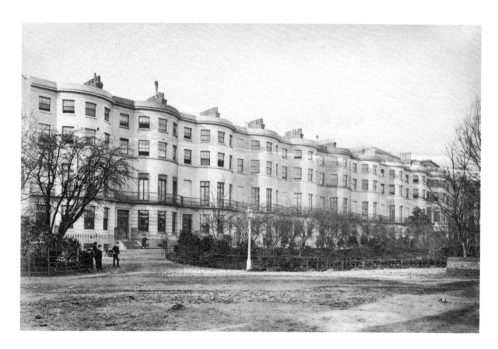

The Homes of the 'Forty Thieves'

Liverpool Terrace was built on London Fields in the early nineteenth century. It is one of the oldest and most attractive streets in Worthing. Across the small park, which once contained archery butts and a bowling green, is the looming bulk of the Montague shopping centre fronted by Elizabeth Frink's sculpted heads. In the late nineteenth century, many of the town's supposedly self-serving lawyers and businessmen, known as the 'forty thieves', lived there.

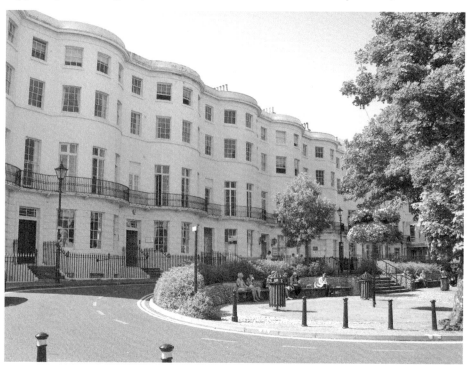

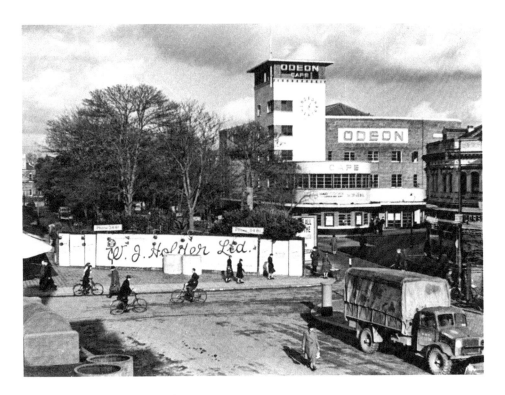

The Odeon and Montague Place

Montague Place was originally a residential area. During the last war, an air-raid shelter was built there and can be seen on the left of this picture. The Odeon cinema was demolished in the 1980s and replaced by a shopping centre. What looks like a bandstand is, instead, a seating area and the large brick wall on the right is the side of the former Woolworth's building. Cheerful with pavement cafés on sunny days, Montague Place looks bleak in winter.

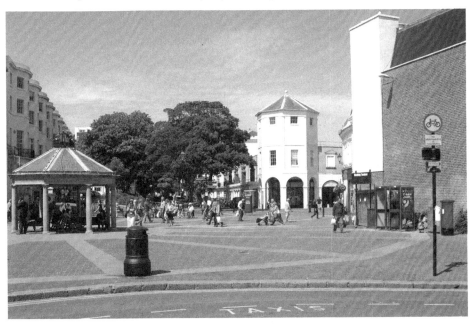

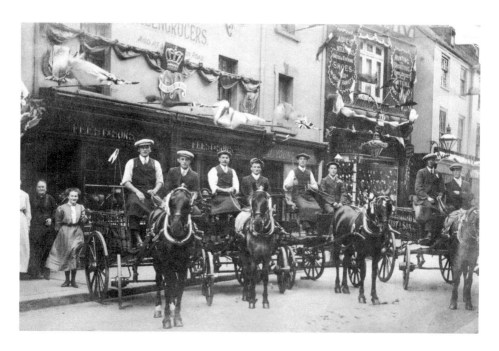

Staff Celebration at Feest & Sons

Feest & Sons were well-known traders with a shop in Montague Street, in the heart of commercial Worthing. In this picture, the staff are celebrating the coronation of George V in 1911. Feest's, and many of the other old buildings along Montague Street, have been replaced by stark modern shops. The street is now a pedestrian precinct where shoppers can wander at ease, never pausing to think about the days when horses were the main form of transport.

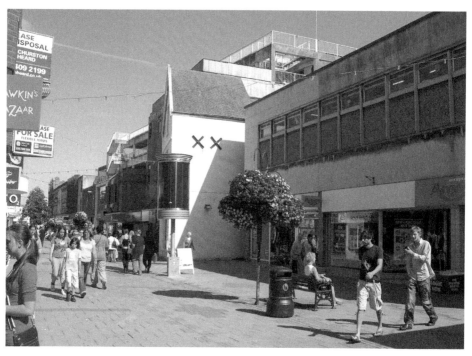

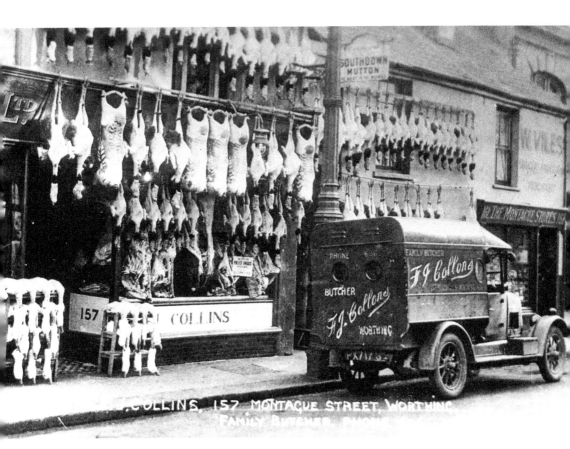

COLLINS, 157 MONTAGUE STREET, WORTHING.
FAMILY BUTCHER. PHONE

Not Simply a Feast for the Eye
Butchers' shops are not what they used to be in 1910 when carcasses could be displayed in serried ranks outside the shop without thought of pollution or contamination. Like many old shops, this one has been demolished to be replaced by a characterless modern block housing one of the town's many charity shops.

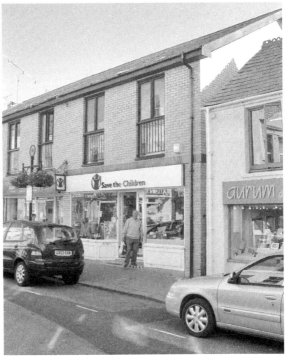

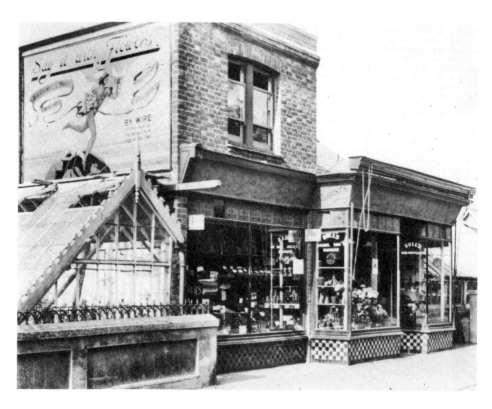

Say It With Flowers

Some slogans last a long time. 'Say it with flowers' was being used by Barnwell's in Crescent Road in the 1920s and is still being used by florists today. It was difficult to work out exactly where Barnwell's had their shop, but this picture gives an idea of how much the upper part of Crescent Road has changed.

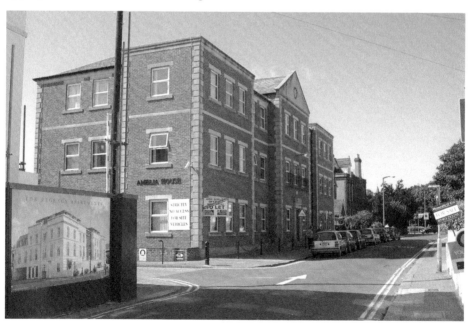

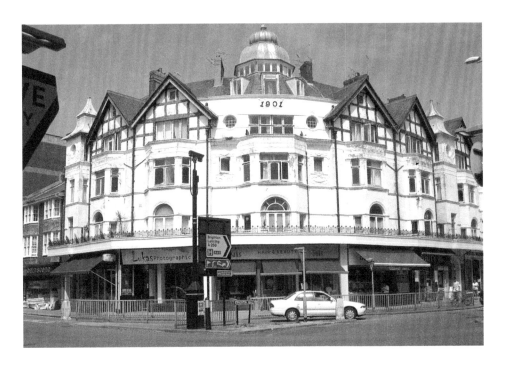

Edwardian Shopping

The Broadway in Brighton Road is typical of the rows of shops and flats that were built around the country in the Edwardian period with the date of its building proudly displayed in moulded plaster. It had become run down but quite a lot of work has been done on it recently, making it smarter than it has been for years. The decorative railings on the left are part of Colonnade House on the corner of Warwick Street.

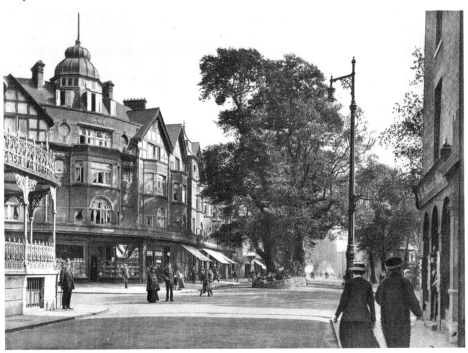

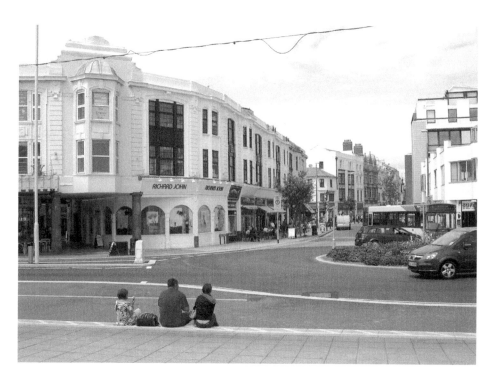

Elegant Shopping 1920s Style

The south-west corner of South Street has changed little since the Arcade was built in the 1920s on the site of the Sea House Hotel. When this picture was taken in *c.* 1935, the streets had been decorated, crowds had gathered and a microphone had been set up on the pier steps, but the cause of their celebration is unknown.

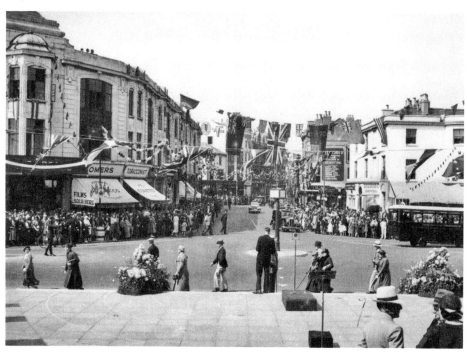

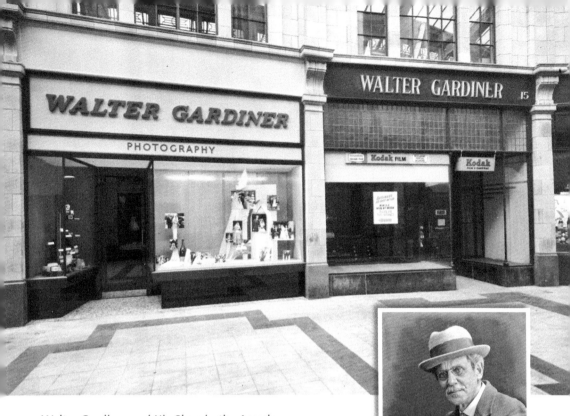

Walter Gardiner and His Shop in the Arcade

The interior of the Arcade is covered with tiles. Walter
Gardiner had a studio in the Broadway but opened this one
in the Arcade in the 1920s. He was clearly expanding into
a second shop where work was ongoing. He was one of the
town's earliest and most respected photographers. He and
his successors took many of the photos in this book. As this
picture shows, many of the shops in the Arcade are now empty.

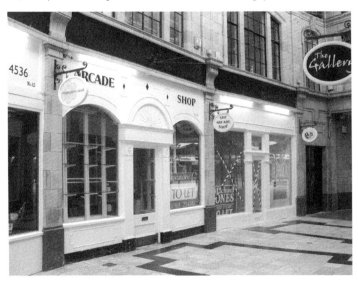

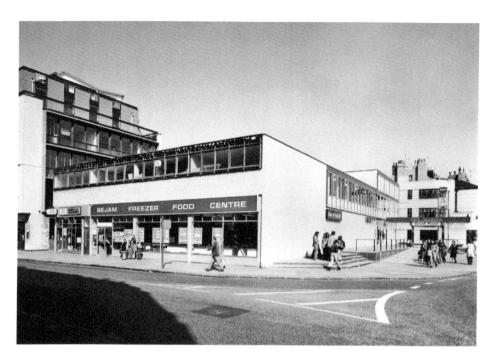

An 'Icy Corner'

Opposite the Arcade, the buildings have changed several times. In 1965, the old Marine Hotel was pulled down and the Bejam frozen food shop and Umbrella Barbeque were built. Since then, the buildings have been altered and Iceland has replaced Bejam – still selling frozen food. During the Great Storm of October 1987, the windows in this building were blown out, spreading glass all over the street.

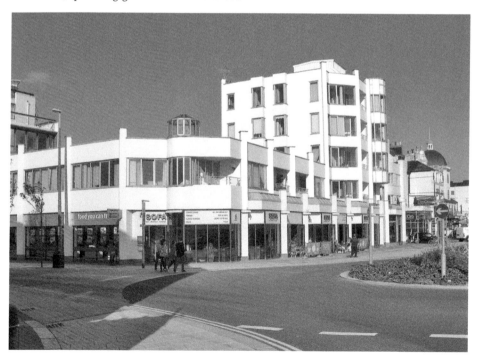

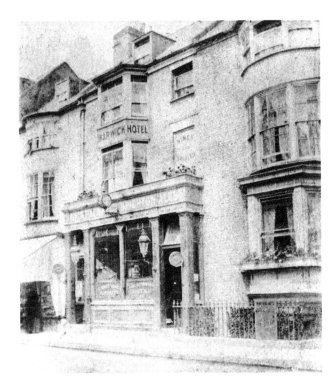

The Warwick Hotel
In 1902, the Warwick Hotel in Warwick Street advertised that it sold Chapman and Brighton Ales. By 2009, it had been renamed the Warwick, the frontage had been brightly painted and, since Warwick Street had been pedestrianised, customers were able to sit outside to enjoy a drink.

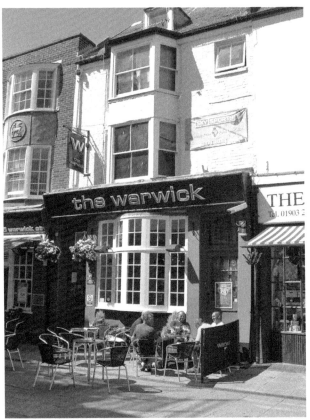

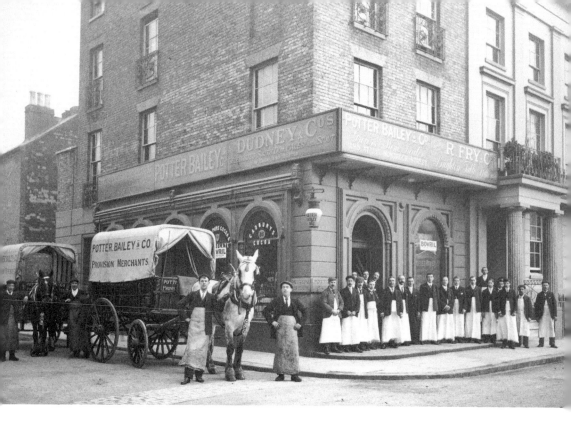

Potter, Bailey & Co.'s All-Male Staff

Potter, Bailey & Co. were the largest grocer's in Victorian Worthing with premises on the corner of Ann Street and the High Street. The late-Victorian staff are all lined up outside, smartly dressed. The signs show that their stock included ales, stout, Bovril and cocoa. Sadly, this building, and its neighbours, have been replaced by a utilitarian multi-storey car park.

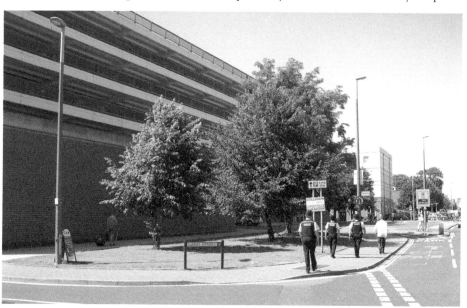

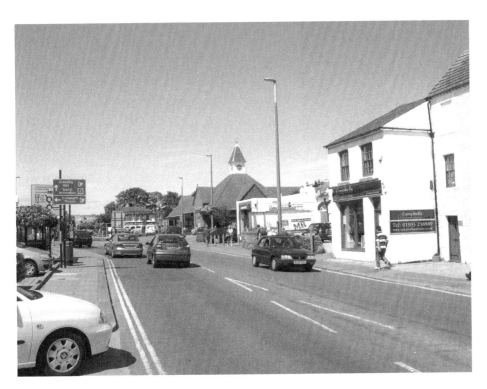

The Northern High Street is Regularly Redeveloped

The High Street has been the site of repeated redevelopment. By the 1970s, earlier houses had been replaced by Searle's Garage. At the far left is the Anchor pub, now called the Jack Horner. The garage site was later redeveloped as Safeways and is still occupied by a supermarket, the more upmarket Waitrose. The small building in the foreground is still there.

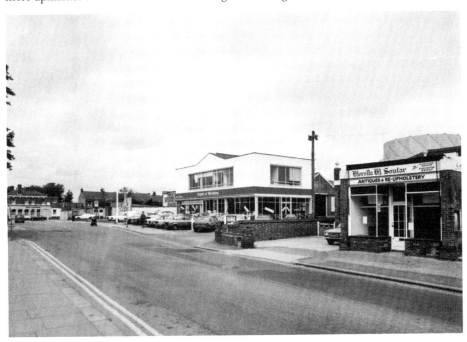

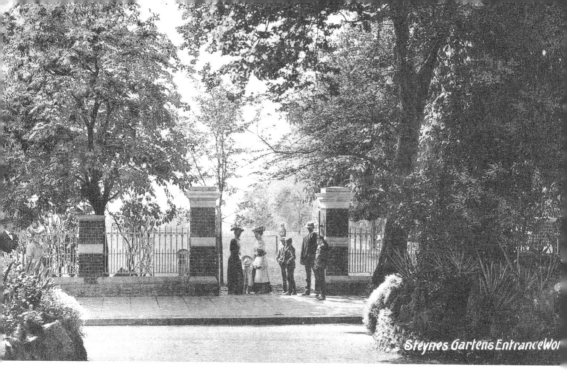

Steynes Gardens Entrance Wor

Steyne Gardens From the North

Steyne Gardens, between the Broadway and the seafront was once fully enclosed by railings and fronted by mature trees. This picture looks south from the northern entrance in *c.* 1905. Today, the gardens are much more open, bordered by low walls and in spite of the trees, little more than an open grassy area where people like to relax.

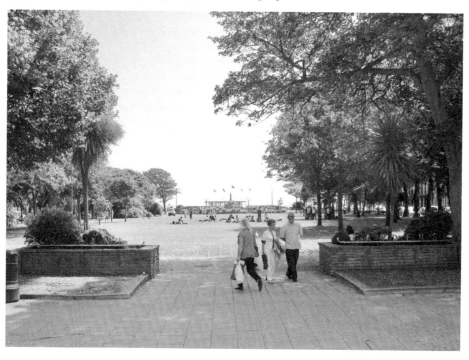

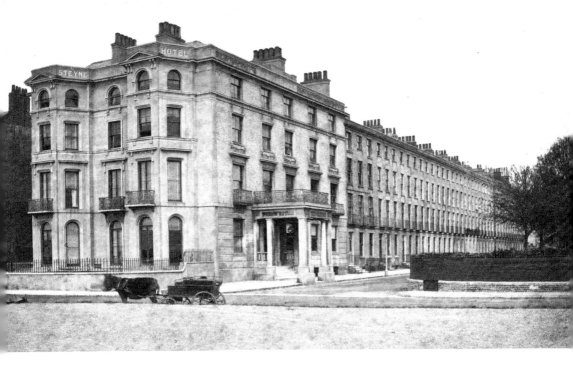

One of the Oldest Hotels in Town
The buildings that housed the Steyne Hotel and lined Steyne Gardens have changed little since this picture was taken in *c.* 1893. The near end is now a restaurant while most of the other buildings are now the Chatsworth Hotel.

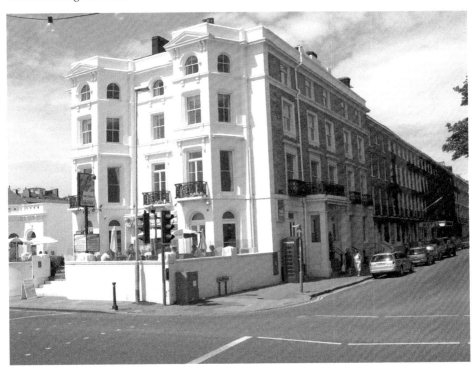

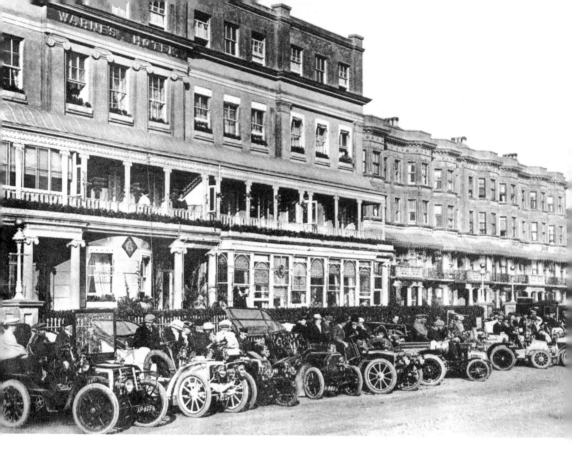

The End of Warne's Was the End of an Era

Warne's, Worthing's finest hotel, where Emperor Haile Selassie of Ethiopia once lived, was targeted for redevelopment in the 1980s. Tragically, it then suffered two serious fires, which meant that the listed building could not be saved. After the hotel was demolished, the site lay empty before being redeveloped as luxury flats. The modern picture shows that the Eardley, which once stood beside Warne's, has now been demolished in its turn and new apartments will be built on the site.

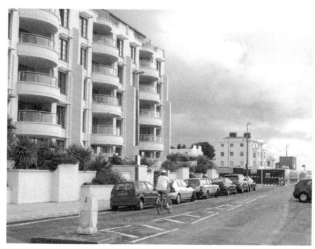

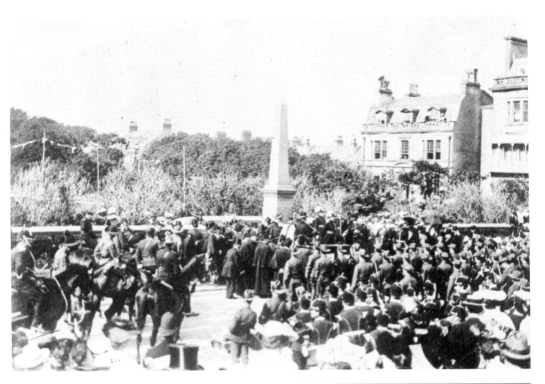

Commemorative Obelisk in Steyne Gardens

Worthing's memorial to the men who died in the South African Wars was unveiled at the southern end of Steyne Gardens in 1903. This picture shows the crowd watching the unveiling. The contrast between the backdrop to the memorial then and now is stark.

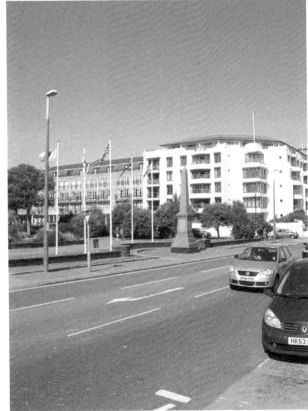

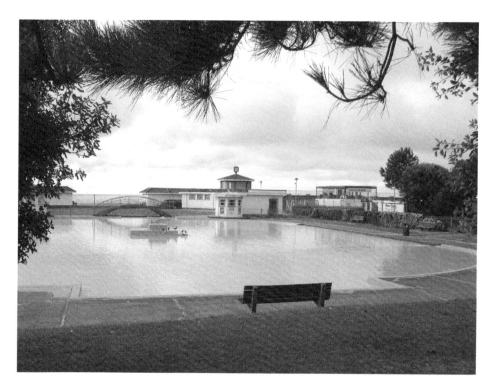

War and Peace – Barbed Wire and the Children's Pool

The paddling pool near Peter Pan's Playground was just one of the many areas of Worthing closed during the war. In this picture, coils of barbed wire that had been removed from the seafront lie piled up near the pool. As the modern picture shows, the pool was later restored to its former glory and it remains an enticing and popular spot for families to go on warm days and is rarely this peaceful.

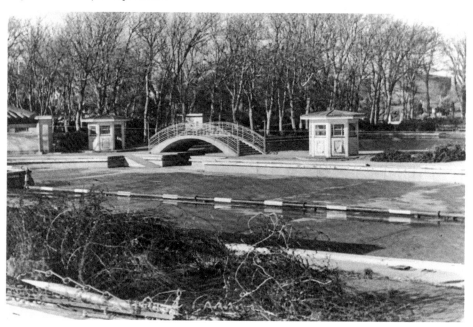

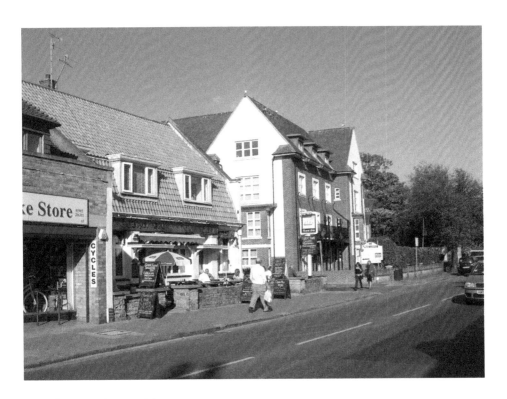

Convalescence in Worthing

This attractive Victorian building on the corner of Brighton Road and Park Road was being used as a convalescent home when this picture, showing both nurses and patients, was taken. Later, it became the John Horniman School. It was demolished in the early 2000s and was replaced by an anonymous block of flats.

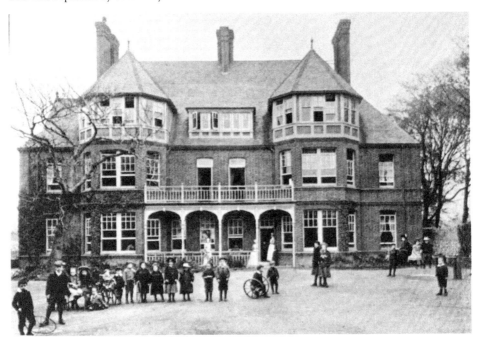

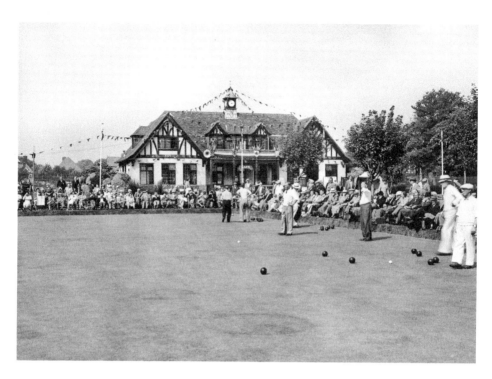

The Home of English Bowls

Beach House Park is the home of the English Bowls Association and has been the site of many tournaments, such as those shown in these two pictures taken over fifty years apart. The building itself has changed little and is still known for its velvet greens.

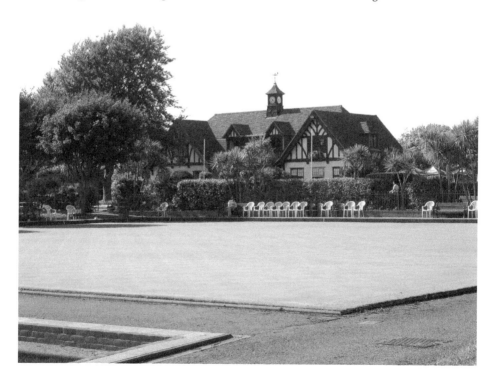

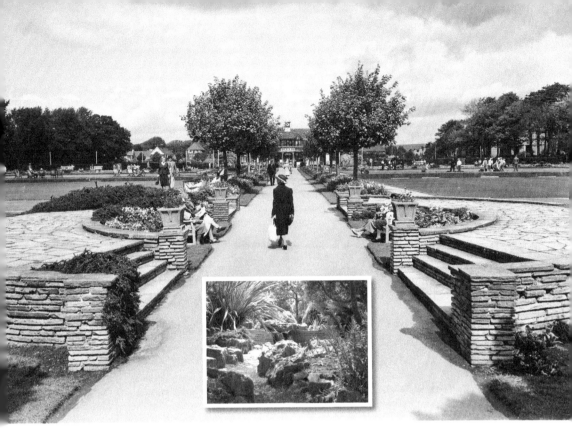

Where is the Pigeons' War Memorial?

Beach House park is also known for its glorious flowerbeds. As the inset picture shows, it is also the site of Britain's only war memorial dedicated to carrier pigeons, which was the brainchild of local writer Nancy Price and which was opened in 1949.

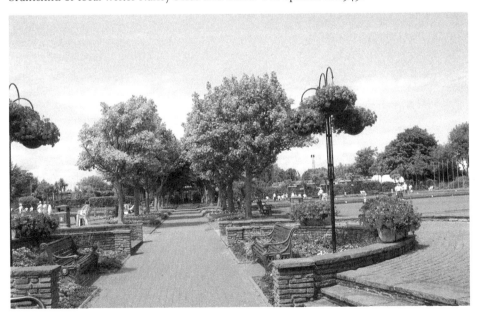

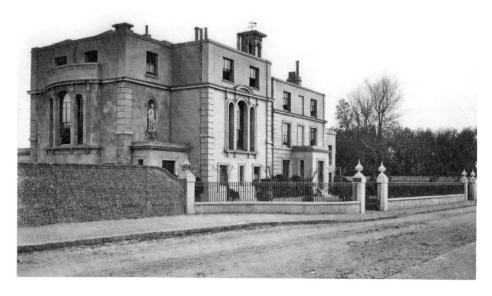

The Aquarena on Brighton Road

Facing Brighton Road, Beach House and Beachfield were elegant early-Victorian villas. Beach House survives but Beachfield was demolished in 1961 and the Aquarena was built in its place. Controversial plans for redeveloping the Aquarena have recently been put forward. This picture was taken in around 1901, when the Brighton Road was still quiet, and not jammed with traffic.

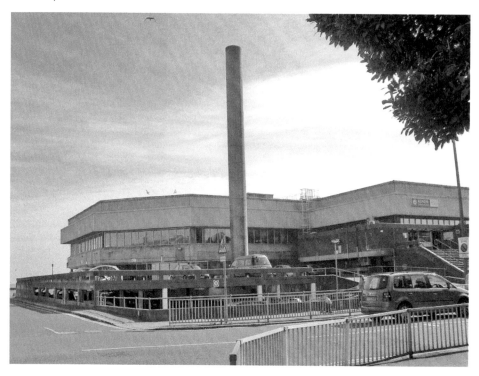

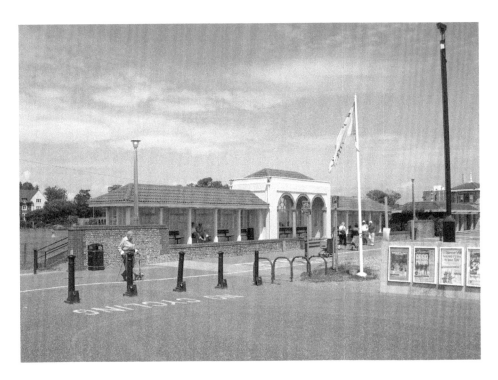

Sheltering From the Sea Breeze

Denton Gardens were created in 1924 near Splash Point at the eastern end of the seafront. At the southern end of the gardens, a row of shelters was built, which, though showing its age, is still happily occupied, presumably by the same sort of people who have beach huts at the other end of town. Apparently, they were recently threatened by redevelopment but it is to be hoped that they will be preserved. Don't miss the penny-in-the-slot weighing machine by the wall.

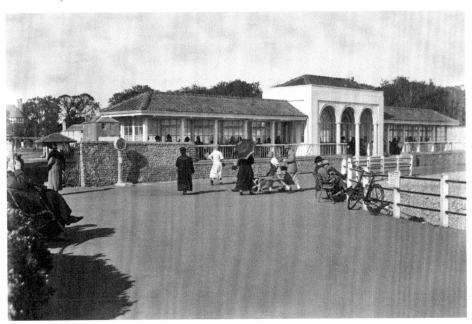

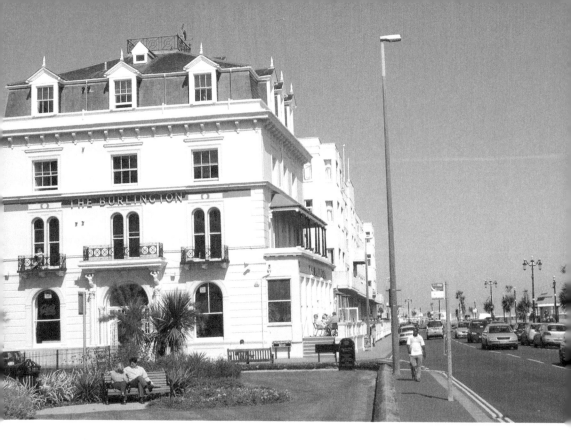

Where Better to Enjoy a Drink and a Sea View?

Happily, the Burlington Hotel still graces the seafront as it has done since 1865. First called the West Worthing Hotel, it was renamed the Burlington in 1890 and is at the eastern end of Heene Terrace. It is pleasing to see that it still has a popular terrace facing the sea as it did in this picture taken *c*. 1925.

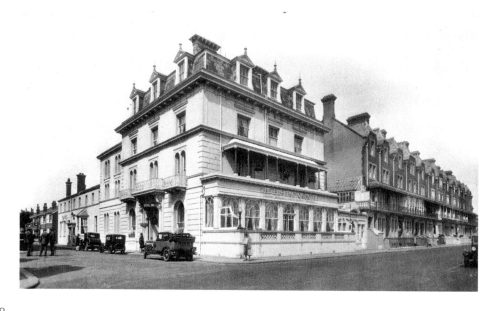

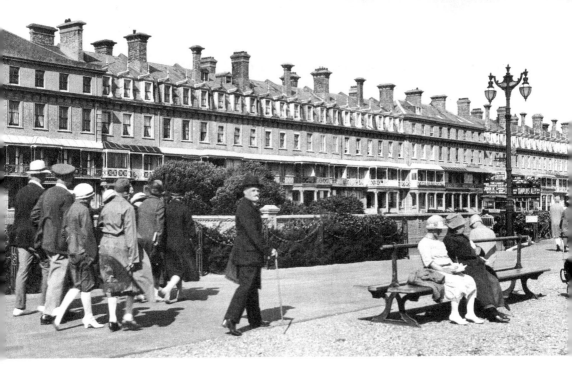

Grand Building in Heene, West of Worthing

The elegant Heene Terrace was built in the mid-nineteenth century, when Heene was still separate from Worthing. This picture, looking at the Terrace across the promenade in around 1930, does not show the beautiful flowerbeds that stood in front of the houses. The gardens are simpler than they used to be, but are still beautiful.

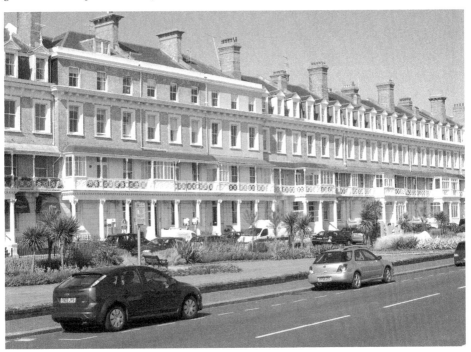

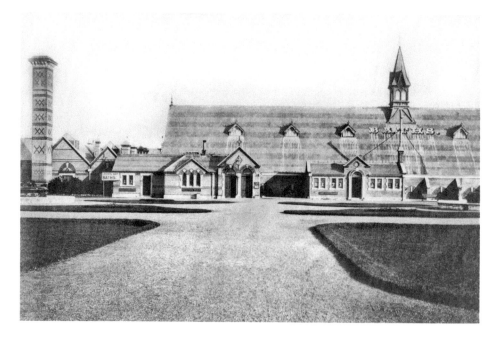

The Aquatic Centre and Pleasure Grounds in Heene

Heene Baths, just around the corner from Heene Terrace, were Worthing's first public swimming baths offering salt, freshwater and seaweed baths as well as the chance to use the main pool. They opened in 1865 and were hailed as being among the finest in the country. Pleasure grounds and a roller-skating rink were later added. The whole complex was demolished in 1973 and the offices of an insurance company were built on the site.

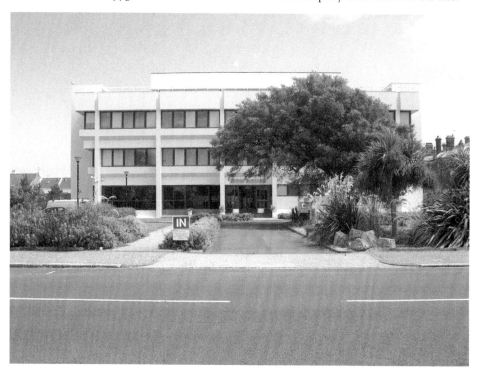

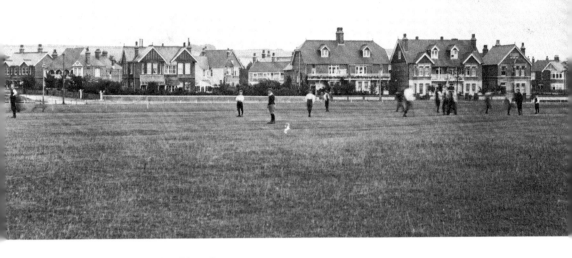

Broadwater, Worthing's Older Sister

Broadwater, now a suburb of Worthing, was once its larger neighbour. Many of the larger houses were built around the Green. Dated 1910, this picture shows children playing on the Green. It is now edged by tall trees and remains important for cricket, football, seasonal funfairs and general relaxation.

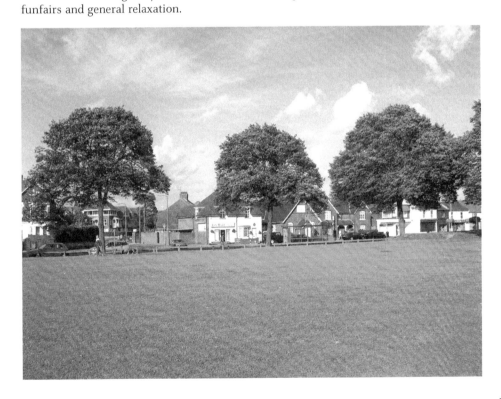

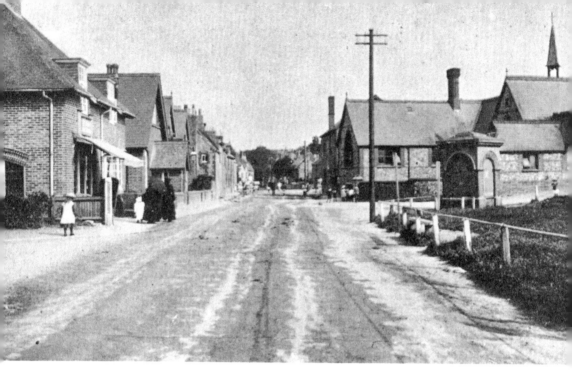

Not a Cart or Car in Sight

This picture is taken looking towards the centre of Broadwater from the Green. The drinking fountain and the village school are on the right of the picture. It is hard to imagine this picture, with the un-metalled road and no pavements, was only taken a hundred years ago.

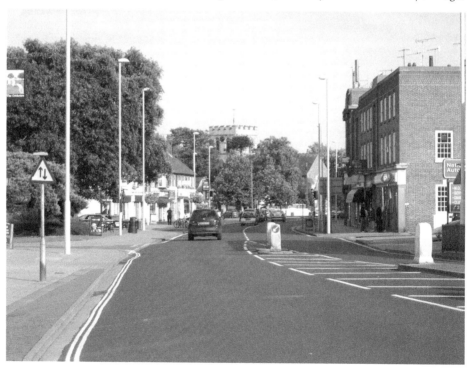

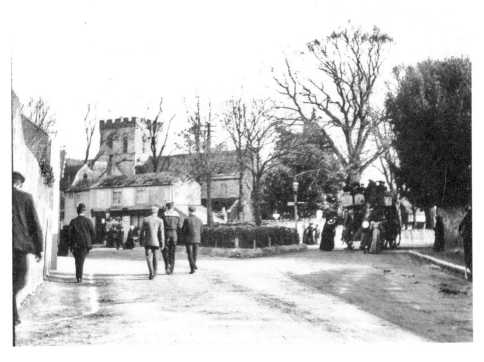

Broadwater Church and Triangle

Looking towards Broadwater church in around 1900, this picture shows the green triangle that used to be at the junction between the main road and Broadwater Street East. This junction is now very busy with parked cars and shops lining the road on both sides.

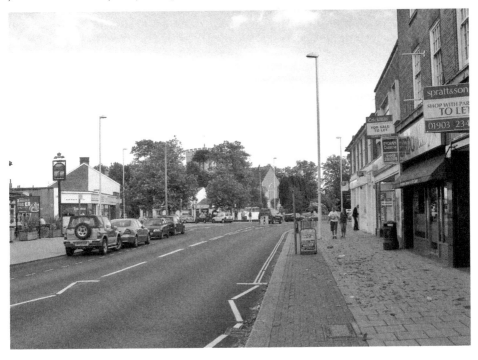

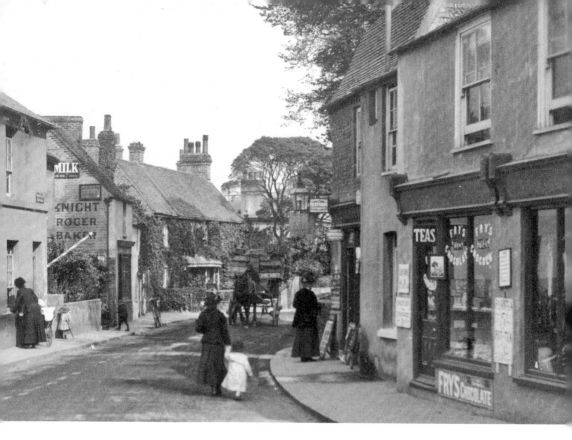

The Heart of the Old Village

In the early twentieth century, the buildings at the top of Broadwater Street East were a mixture of houses and shops, including Pollicutt's tobacco and stationery shop. Today, there is still a mixture of houses and shops.

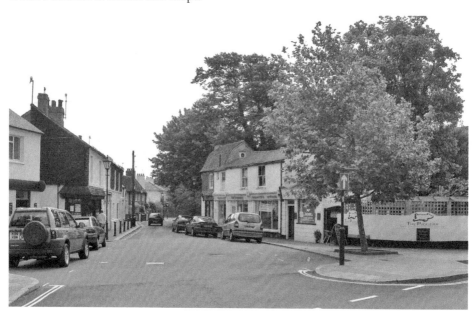

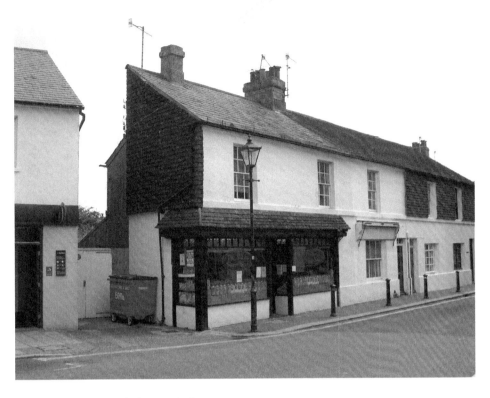

Sweets Never Lose Their Popularity

Luff's sweet shop was on the northern side of Broadwater Street East in the early twentieth century. The picture is labelled 'The Celebrated Broadwater Sweet Shop Near Worthing'. By a nice turn of fate, although many other people have occupied the property over the years, it is once again a sweet shop.

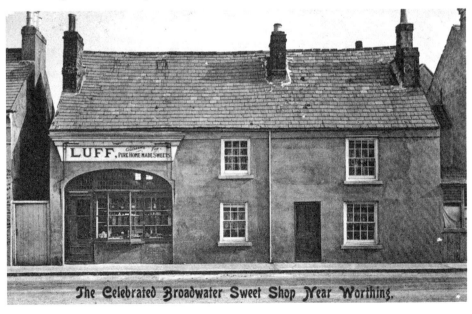

LUFF, PURE HOME MADE SWEETS

The Celebrated Broadwater Sweet Shop Near Worthing.

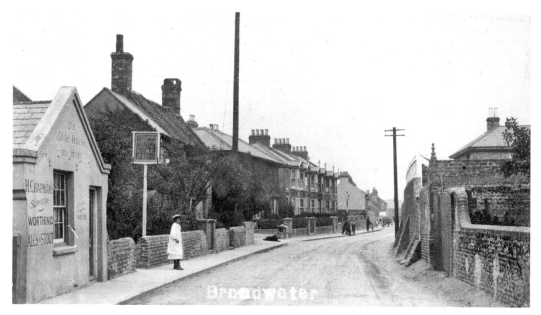

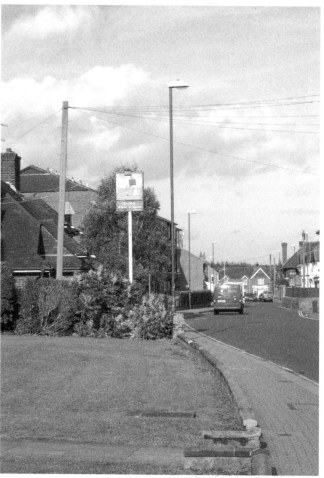

One of the Oldest Pubs in the Village

Further east, Broadwater Street East in the 1920s was a quiet residential road with a pub, The Old House at Home. The buildings in the foreground of the older picture have been demolished and flats built on the site, fronted by grass, but the pub is still thriving.

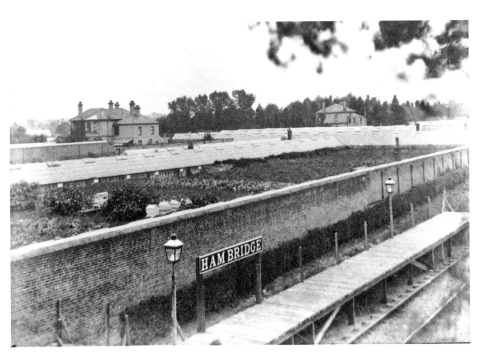

Someone is Always Watching You

Ham Bridge Halt, was renamed West Worthing Station in 1949. Many of Worthing's famous nurseries were concentrated in this area and some of the Maybush Nursery glasshouses can be seen in this picture. The nursery closed in 1915. The simple station has been replaced by one where security lights, high fences and CCTV cameras are considered essential.

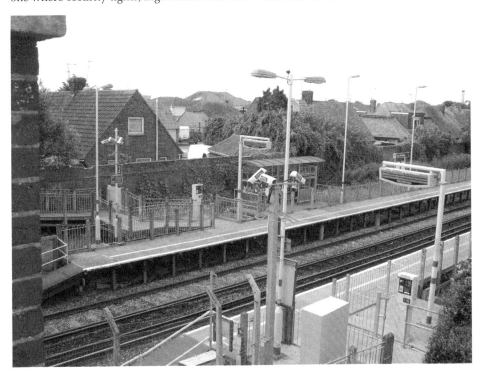

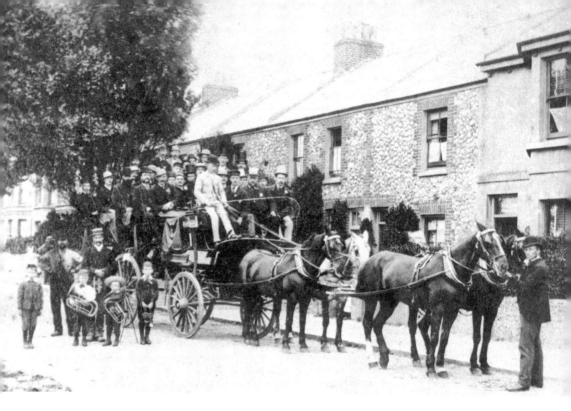

A Day Away From the Glasshouses

Nurseries employed large numbers of men in the late nineteenth century. This picture shows a group of nurserymen gathered outside cottages in Ham Road in their Sunday best ready to go on their annual outing. Members of the Duffield family are carrying their musical instruments. The cottages in Ham Road have not been changed much since this picture was taken.

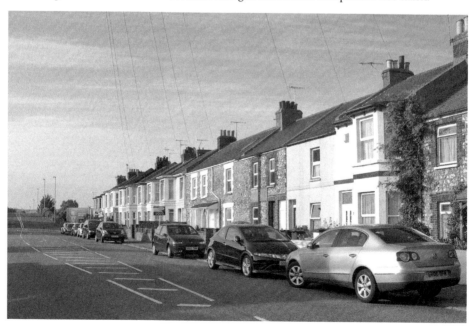

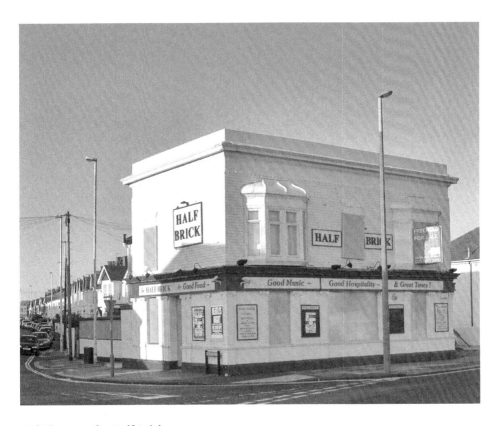

Sad Times at the Half Brick

The Half Brick in this picture from 1910 is not the original pub, which was washed away and had to be rebuilt further from the sea in 1874. Its fortunes have varied over the years but appear to have hit rock bottom as the pub is boarded up and is for sale.

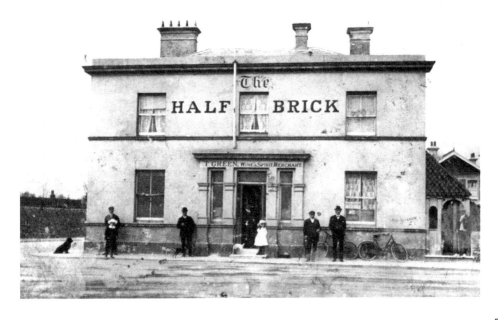

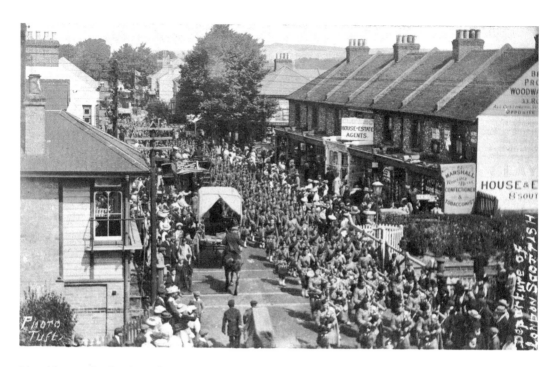

Marching to the Station After Manoeuvres

In the early twentieth century, numerous regiments came to Sussex on manoeuvres. In 1907, the London Scottish left their training camp and marched down South Street, Tarring, towards the station, accompanied by their pipers and watched by a small crowd. The soldiers may have gone, but South Street is still busy, with regular delays when the level-crossing gates are closed.

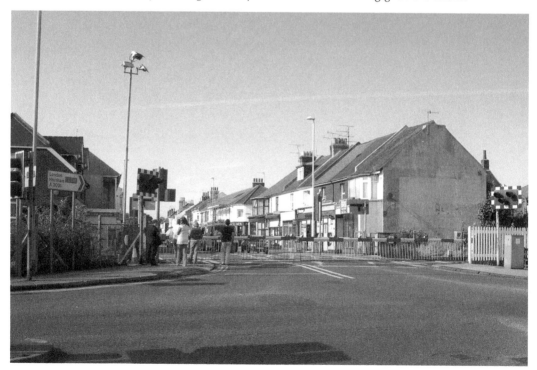

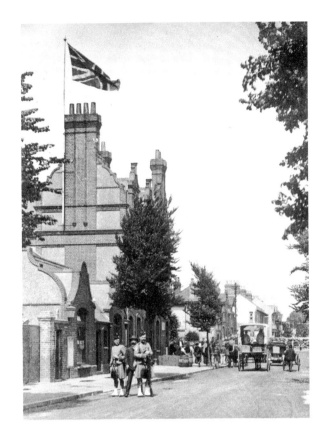

Tarring Crossing and the Downview Hotel
The soldiers beside the Downview Hotel, just south of Tarring crossing, in this picture, are wearing kilts and may be part of the London Scottish, who we know were on manoeuvres here before the First World War. Little has changed in this area apart from the number of streetlights and cars.

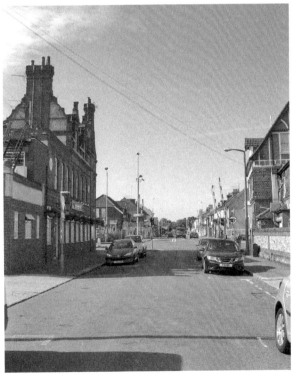

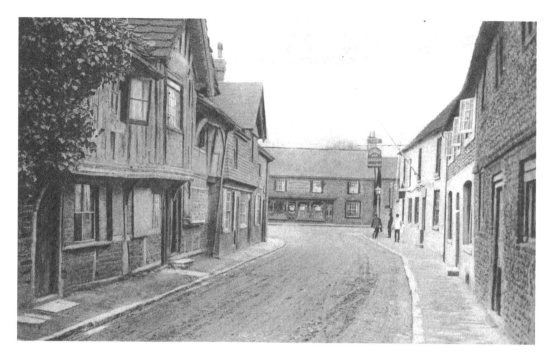

A Taste of Medieval Tarring

The main difference between these photos taken in 1907 and 2009 is the number of cars. The High Street in Tarring is a very narrow road, lined with very old buildings, the stars of which are undoubtedly the medieval Parsonage Row Cottages, seen on the left. The George and Dragon public house is on the right.

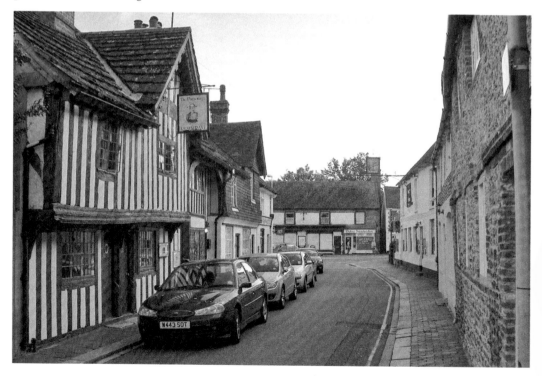

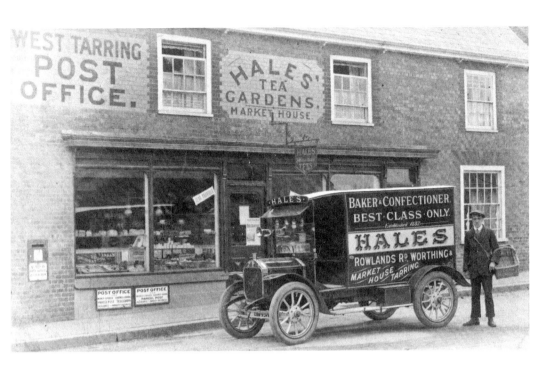

An Unfortunate Situation

It is a sad sign of the times that the Tarring Post Office, which was thriving in 1920, is now closed. It is to be hoped that someone will be able to reopen it as a business of some kind. The delivery van comes from Hales Bakery, who appear to have had premises in Tarring and in Rowlands Road.

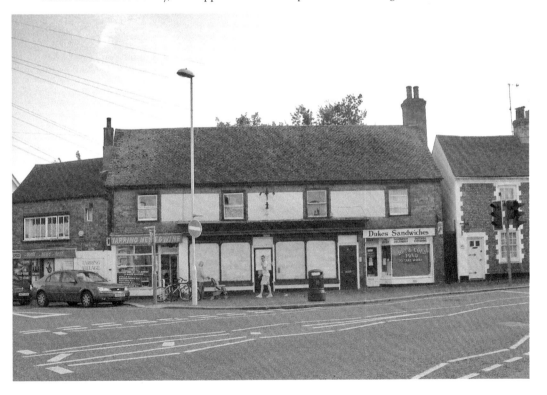

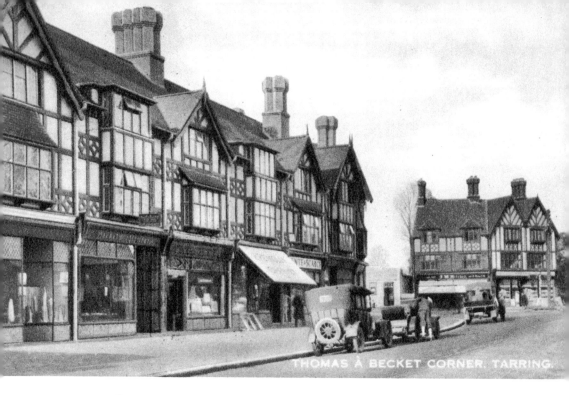

Thomas À Becket Corner in the 1930s
Even in the early days of motoring Thomas À Becket Corner was an important junction, though, as these four cars show, it was hardly congested. The junction is named after the pub, which still stands there beside the mock-Tudor splendour of the other buildings. Today, the traffic is controlled by traffic lights and there are long queues in busy times.

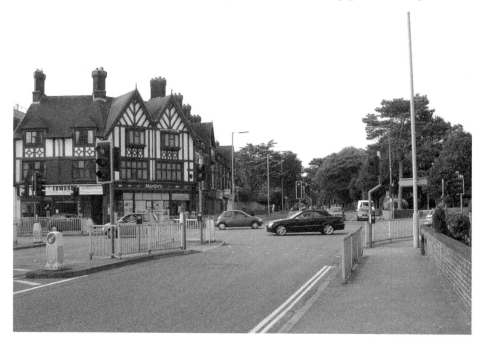

84

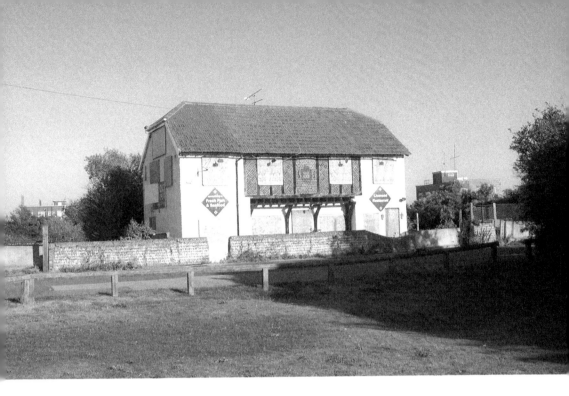

Goring Beach Shop in the Second World War
The Old Provisions Shop near the beach at Sea Place, Goring, later became Baloo's restaurant. Part of a penny-in-the-slot weighing machine can be seen in front of the mock-Tudor building. The signs advertise the fact that they sold tobacco, newspapers, provisions, fruit and grocery items. Although it has been altered, the building is clearly recognisable. Sadly, it is now closed and its fate is unclear.

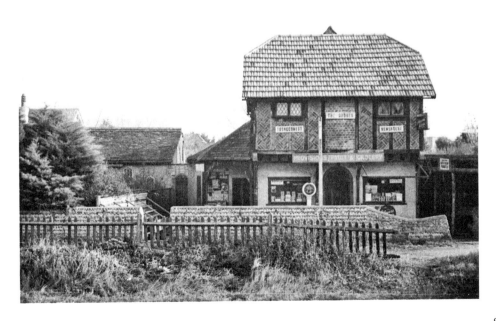

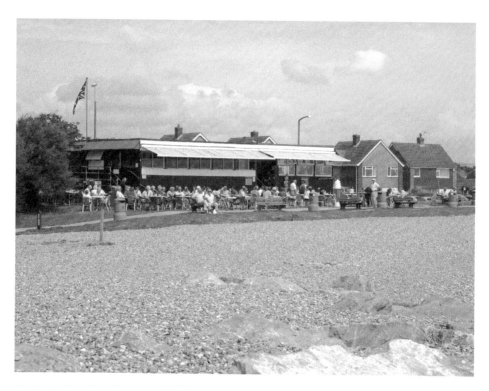

Probably the Most Famous Café in Sussex
People travel long distances to visit the Sea Lane Café on the edge of the beach at Goring and to buy fish from the fishermen. The crude hut that was the café in the 1930s has long since been replaced, but the café is still essentially a simple place where crowds flock to eat, drink and relax throughout the year, watching the sea and surfers no matter what the weather is like.

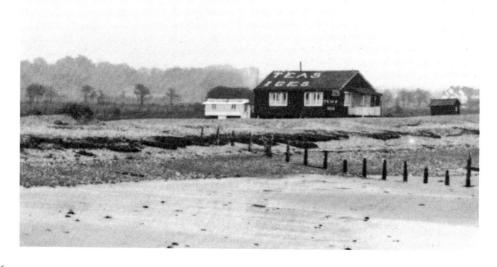

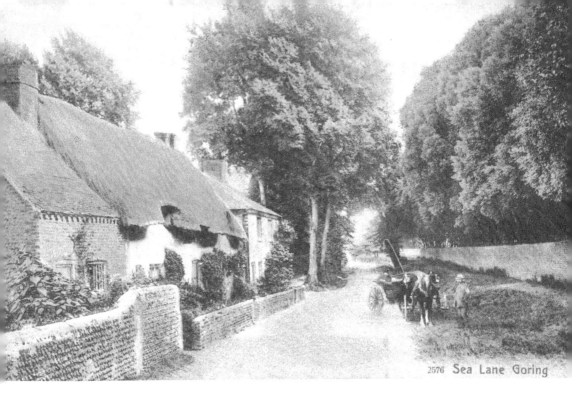

2576 Sea Lane Goring

Bungalow-land Amid the Ilexes

Sea Lane, Goring, still has plenty of ilex trees but almost everything else in Sea Lane has changed since the older photograph was taken in the early twentieth century. A bungalow has replaced the thatched cottage, the road has been widened and metalled to cope with the volume of cars that use it, pavements have been added and some of the trees have been cut down. Driving up the dual carriageway today, it is hard to imagine Sea Lane as it used to be.

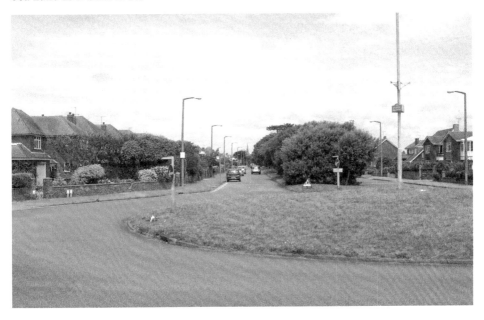

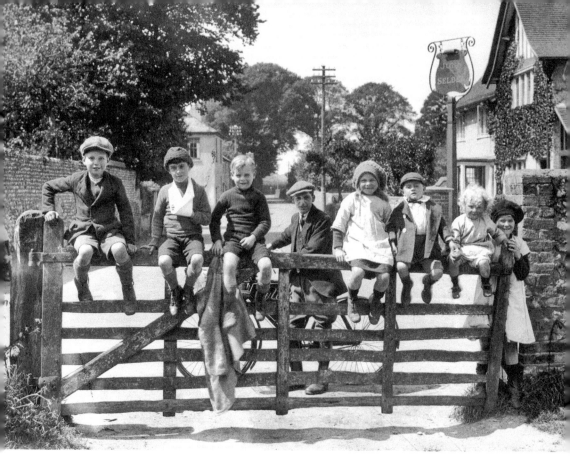

Only Part of the Wyatt Family

This cheerful bunch are six of the eight children born to Harry and Alice Wyatt, sitting on a gate at the junction of Salvington Road and Half Moon Lane. The pub in the background is the John Selden, named after a famous local philosopher, and still in business. Pescoe (Percy) Wyatt has his hand in a sling. The identity of the man with the bike is not known. As might be expected, the scene looks much more built up than it did in 1920.

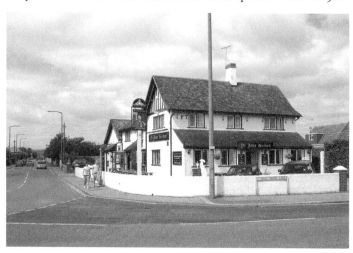

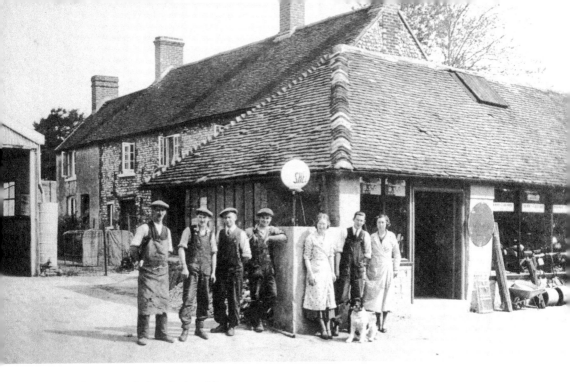

Every Village Needed a Blacksmith

Overington's Garage, Forge and Ironmongers was a fixture in Salvington Road until quite recently, mending and servicing machinery such as lawnmowers as well as selling a wide range of useful bits and pieces. This picture shows the family with members of their staff outside the shop in the 1930s. Their forge and shop have now been converted into accommodation.

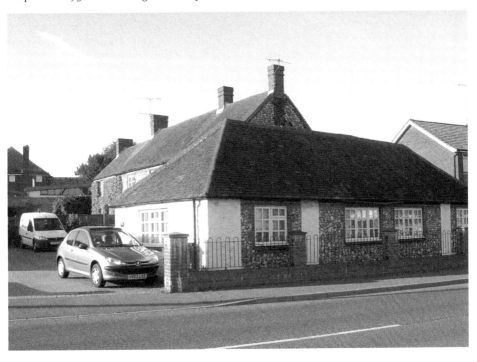

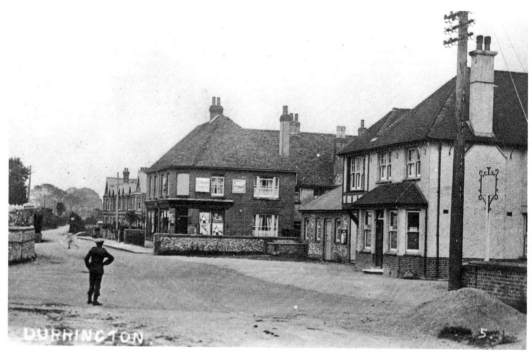

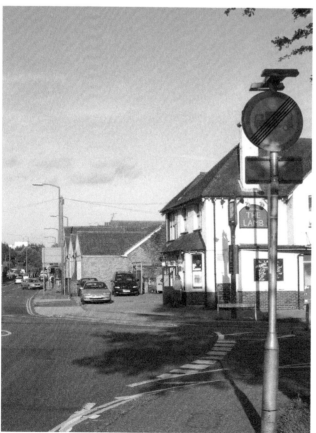

Salvington Village in the 1920s
The Lamb Inn on Salvington
Road now faces a roundabout
instead of a quiet lane, judging
by the man standing in the
middle of the road. To the left
of the pub is the shop and post
office and beyond that, Rock
Cottages. Since this was taken,
the shop has been rebuilt.

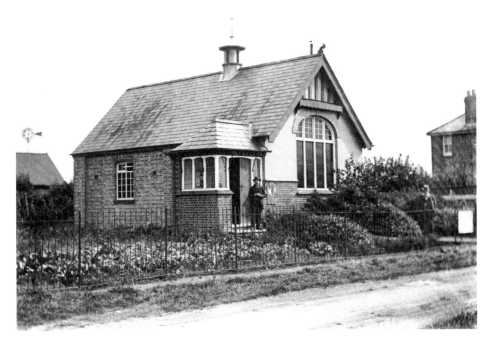

The New Church in Durrington

Durrington Free Church was built on Salvington Road in 1912, when it stood in a sizeable plot. The identities of the two men standing by the church soon after the opening is not known. Cottages have been built close to the church on the near side. Behind it, several extensions have been added to house its growing congregation and its coffee shop. It is now known as the New Life Church.

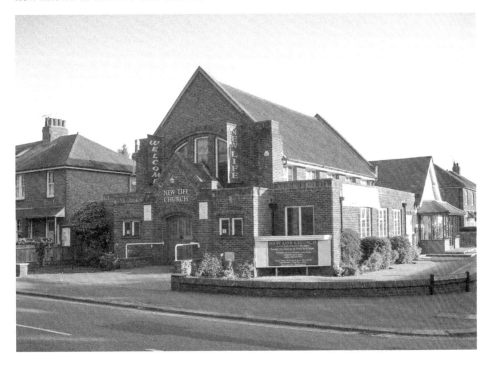

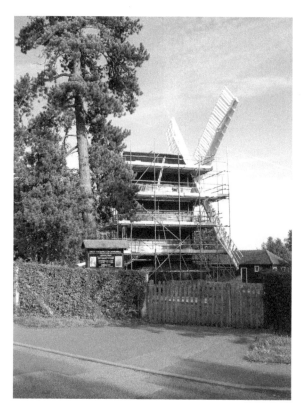

The Only Mill Left Standing
Salvington Windmill is the only mill to survive in the Worthing area. High on a hill to the north of the town, it was a working mill until 1897 and occasionally ground flour until 1914. After that, the mill fell into disrepair. Luckily, a team of skilful volunteers lovingly restored it. The mill now grinds corn again and is open to the public on selected weekends throughout the summer. As with any mill, maintenance is a never-ending task.

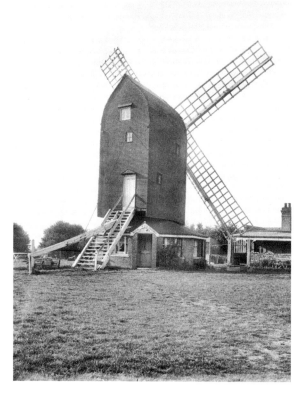

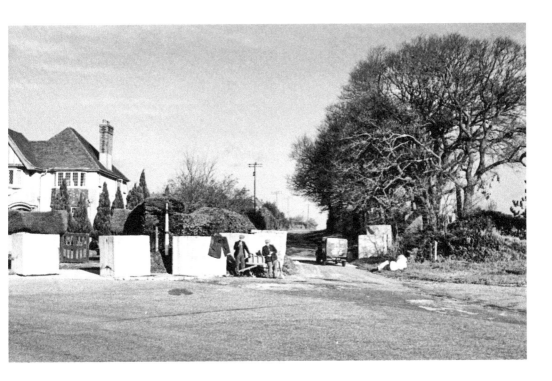

Ready for the Enemy in the 1940s

Workmen with a handcart at the junction of Mill Lane and Arundel Road, High Salvington. One of them has hung his jacket on one of the concrete 'tank traps'. House owners along Arundel Road have suffered from a series of plans to widen the road, none of which has materialised. The house is currently for sale; perhaps the owners have had enough of the traffic and uncertainty.

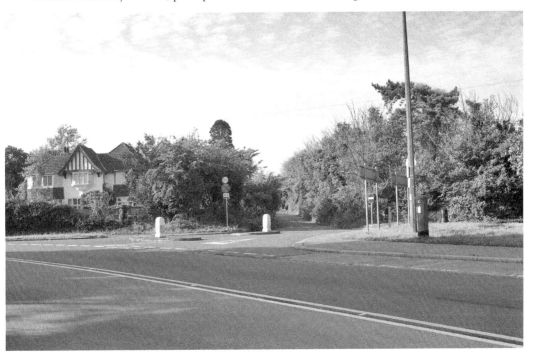

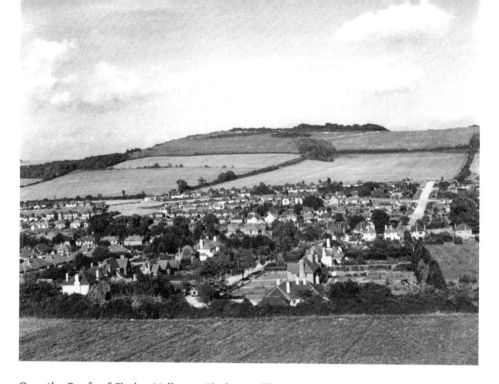

Over the Roofs of Findon Valley to Cissbury Hill Fort

House-building in Findon Valley progressed very fast from the 1920s and had begun to reach up the lower slopes of Cissbury hill fort by the 1950s. Luckily, the importance of the Downland was then recognised and further building was prevented. The view from the Gallops west of the A24 shows just how far development had spread.

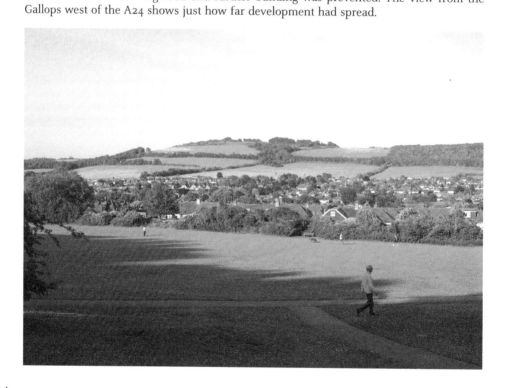

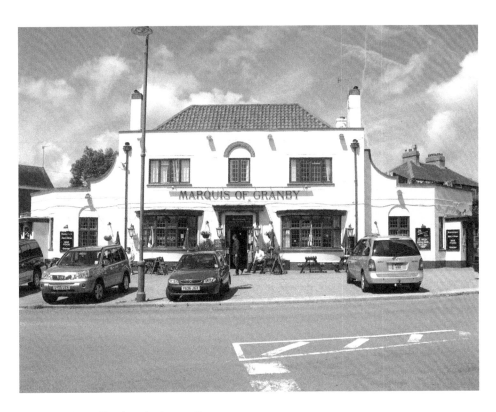

The Proud Landlord and His Family

Sompting village is tiny, but has two pubs. One of them is the Marquis of Granby. In this picture, the landlord, Abraham Duffield, is standing on the front step with his wife, daughter and dog. Since this picture was taken in the 1920s, the pub has been remodelled. During the works, the remains of a Roman burial were uncovered and are on display in Worthing Museum.

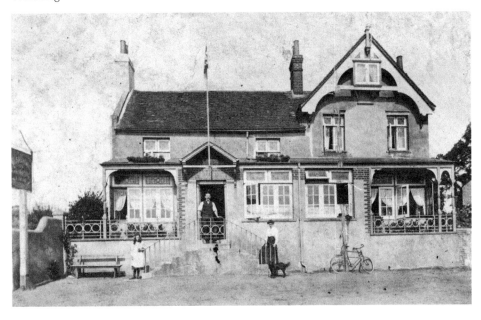

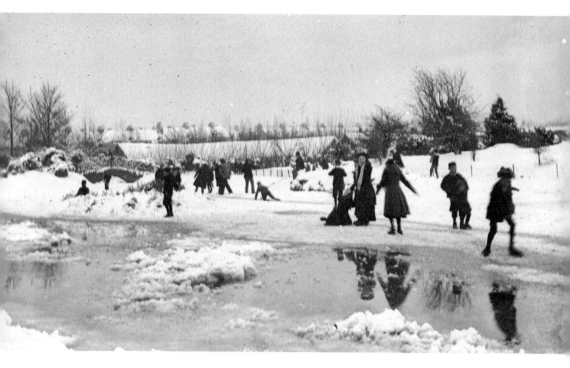

Skating in Homefield Park in 1894.

Acknowledgements

I would like to thank Martin Hayes, Local Studies Librarian for West Sussex, for his support. The Local Studies Collections kept at Worthing Library are invaluable and have grown significantly due to his hard work and enthusiasm. With Martin's help, I was able to select the old photographs for this book from the West Sussex Past Pictures website at www.westsussexpast.org.uk. Over 11,000 images from the 1840s to the present, provided by the County Library Service and local museums, can be viewed, downloaded and used for educational or private use free of charge. Photographic-quality prints can be ordered too. It follows, too, that I am grateful to everyone who has contributed to this amazing resource.

I am very grateful to Elda Elliott for her friendship and steadfast support.

Whenever I write anything, my mother provides enthusiasm, support and proofreading. She also provides enjoyable 'time out' from work and makes everything easier than it would otherwise be.

My cat, Barney, should not be forgotten; his companionship is invaluable, though his tendency to sit on my piles of papers is deplorable.